23

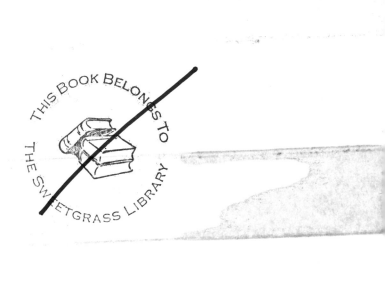

DEVERON to DEVASTATION

DEVERON to DEVASTATION

BROTHER OFFICERS OF THE 7TH ROYAL INNISKILLING FUSILIERS IN THE FIRST WORLD WAR

JAMES FRASER BOURHILL

FONTHILL

For Jackie

Learn more about Fonthill Media. Join our mailing list to
find out about our latest titles and special offers at:
www.fonthillmedia.com

Fonthill Media Limited
www.fonthillmedia.com
office@fonthillmedia.com

First published in the United Kingdom 2014

British Library Cataloguing in Publication Data:
A catalogue record for this book is available from the British Library
Copyright © James Bourhill 2014

ISBN 978-1-78155-354-1

Typeset in 10.5pt on 13pt Sabon LT Std
Printed and bound by CPI Group (UK) Ltd, Croydon, CR0 4YY

Contents

Acknowledgements

What inspired me to write this book was the diary of A. D. Reid—not only its content, but also its existence as an historical artefact. I am grateful to everyone whose hands it passed through, for recognizing its value and safeguarding it for future generations.

In my research, I was fortunate to have the assistance of the Memorial Museum Passchendaele 1917, which is at Zonnebeke in Belgium. Steven Vandenbussche was a goldmine of information. George Stephens, an old Inniskillings man, kindly helped me to find what I needed at the Enneskillen Castle. My thanks to everyone who provided the images to illustrate aspects of the book, especially Gerald Prinsloo of the military archives in Pretoria and Hamish Paterson of the Ditsong Museum of Military History in Johannesburg.

One of the unintended consequences of researching and writing the book was having A. D. Reid's name added to the roll of honour at Westminster School—nearly a century late. For this I have to thank Elizabeth Wells, the school archivist. Nothing enhances the story more than the maps which were drawn by the ever-patient Genevieve Edwards. Above all, I am grateful to Fonthill Media for sharing with me my conviction that this story deserves to be told. A voice which was silenced almost a century ago will now finally be heard.

Introduction

The diary of A. D. Reid, if it can be called a diary, is written in pencil in a brown-covered, field service correspondence book and as will soon become apparent, it was intended for a wider audience. As the diarist himself explained in his first entry, his intention was not to chronicle events—dates were not important to him. In some places, the names of people were left blank, or indicated by initials only. This may be due to security or censorship regulations. Entries were sporadic and there are huge gaps, but each entry is a story in its own right.

From time to time, Reid used his correspondence book for its intended purpose. There is correspondence with the income tax office in London which was insisting that he submit an income tax return for 1916–17, even though he had lived in Canada for five years and paid taxes there. The date was 14 June 1917 and he quite rightly reminded those bureaucrats that it was difficult to tend to business at that particular time. Nonetheless, he filled in the form and returned it to them. The brown notebook also contains lecture notes on the employment of the Vickers machine gun in attack or defence, and there are extensive notes on tactics to be employed in trench raids.

Perhaps the most prevalent theme is Reid's preoccupation with his own mortality. With life so precarious, and death a daily reality, it is quite understandable why this should be so. In a letter dated 7 August 1916, while the Battle of the Somme was raging, he wrote to a fellow officer, who had been declared too old for front line service and had remained in England, requesting him to administer the regimental memorial fund. The proposed committee consisted of Colonel Young, Major Reid himself, Captain Kerr and Father Kelly—the regimental chaplain. Reid expressed the hope that some of the members would still be going after the war was over but at the same time considered it wise to have someone at home to 'keep the thing from falling flat after the war is over if anything happens to the committee out here'.[1] As it turned out, Father Kelly was the only member of that committee to survive the war.

Diarists typically failed to record the things which were most important to them or those things which passing time has made important. Contemporary accounts are also subject to repression of war experience. Paul Fussell refers to a wartime diarist who later commented on his own writings: 'There is nothing to get hold of if you are trying to write a proper historical account of it all. No wonder the stuff slips away mercury-wise from proper historians. No wonder they have to erect artificial structures of one sort or another in its place. No wonder it is those artists who recreate life rather than try to re-capture it who, in one way prove the good historians in the end.'[2]

It was not unusual for a man of A. D. Reid's background to try his hand at creative writing. The Edwardians loved literature. They were more than just literate, they were vigorously literary. Besides the fact that there was little else to do, the appeal of popular education and self-improvement was at its peak. Belief in the educative powers of classical and English literature was pervasive.

This was the age of Oscar Wilde and Mark Twain. James Joyce, the indigent Irish author, shares the same birthday as A. D. Reid, and A. A. Milne was a contemporary at Westminster School. In the soldier's kit, it was not unusual to find copies of *Paradise Lost* by John Milton, *Pilgrim's Progress* or the works of Thomas Hardy which were appreciated for being a reflection of real life. No man would want to die before he had finished reading *Far From the Madding Crowd* or *Tess of the D'Urbervilles*. Sophisticated people were given to quoting Omar Khayyám and Rudyard Kipling.

Kipling, known as 'the poet of the empire', was despised by some for his jingoism. Reid's work was not particularly patriotic but he did demonstrate affection for his regiment. His writings include self-composed soldier's songs. The significance of these barrack ballads is that they capture the mood of men still clinging to life with death lying in wait around the corner.

The war lifted even mediocre literary talent beyond its limitations. The typical British soldier-poet in the First World War was a junior officer from a middle class home whose sensibilities were nurtured by English rural life. Poets like Rupert Brooke used nature as a symbol of hope where the sun, wood and water was fused with the joy of youth and purified by national sacrifice.[3]

Writing poetry comes from a desire to rivet impressions. When a man imagines every moment to be his last, the senses and powers of observation are heightened. Verse has also been used to keep the voices heard, it speaks for the fallen. Soldiers developed their own genre, their soliloquies were often sad or evocative, mostly moving, seldom patriotic or openly pacifist.[4] War poetry is in a sense dialogue with the dead, some was experimental, some conventional or a fusion of the two. Soldier-poets found a language which combined lyricism with realism, bitterness and anger—but even they repressed their feelings. Coming from an age of innocence, there had not yet been a need for a language in which to express such violence, pain and grief.

Because his career as a soldier-poet was cut short, A. D. Reid's work is not coloured by subsequent experience. Death froze the meaning of his life and work. By default he is located in the hallowed company of the likes of Rupert Brook, Julian Grenfell, John McCrae, Isaac Rosenberg and Wilfred Owen, all of whom died in the war. Like them, he shuns the sentimental melodrama of wartime propaganda, he makes no religious references and offers no solutions. The anti-war poetry of the Welsh soldier-poet, Hedd Wynn, was less accessible than some of the better-known works because he wrote in the Welsh language. He was killed on 31 July 1917—the same day as A. D. Reid.

Within the ranks of the 1st Royal Inniskilling Fusiliers, there was a published and well respected Irish poet by the name of Francis Ledwidge. Although he is not a household name outside of Ireland, Ledwidge was acquainted with literary greats the likes of W. B. Yeats, and he made his name first as a 'peasant poet' and then as a 'soldier poet'. He too was killed on 31 July 1917. Incidentally, the 1st Battalion was commanded by a South African, Colonel Sherwood Kelly, who won the VC a few months later.

Every aspiring soldier-poet thought of having his work published, and it would not be unreasonable to assume that A. D. Reid intended his writing for some or other trench magazine—some of his work was in fact published in the regimental magazine *The Sprig of Shillelagh* better known as just *The Sprig*. One of the most successful trench magazines was *The Wipers Times* which contained satire, poetry, reflections and 'in' jokes which would have been lost on people at home. Contributions from readers were encouraged but the flood of bad poetry prompted the following famous editorial:

We regret to announce that an insidious disease is affecting the division, and the result is a hurricane of poetry. Subalterns have been seen with a notebook in one hand, and bombs in the other absently walking near the wire in deep communication with their muse... The Editor would be obliged if a few of the poets would break into prose as the paper cannot live by poems alone.[5]

At the turn of the century, Ireland was an agricultural backwater. Like parts of the industrial north, the West Midlands, the Scottish Lowlands and South Wales it was without a professional stratum and therefore without an officer class. This is how Alex became a senior officer in an Irish regiment. At the beginning of the war, officers had to be gentlemen but the high casualty rate among officers soon changed that. Snobbery still existed—temporary officers who spoke with a grammar school accent were never completely accepted. Half-jokingly, they would be referred to as 'temporary gentlemen'.

It must be pointed out that the story of A. D. Reid and his brother H. F. Reid is not the experience of the ordinary British 'Tommy'. The infantry was mainly drawn from the working class but the common plight of fighting men pulled down some of the barriers of social class. Subalterns and even company commanders liked to refer to themselves as 'common soldiers' in solidarity with 'other ranks'—and to distinguish themselves from the despised staff officers. In death everyone was equal and in the war cemeteries there are no privileges of rank.

The literature of the Great War has long been an area of study. This literature has come to encompass poetry, diaries and journals of participants, autobiography, short stories and novels.[6] Memoirs of the First World War typically follow a conventional pattern. First, there is the perilous journey by both water and land through Étaples up to the ever more menacing line. Second, is the 'crucial struggle' of attack, defence and attrition in the trenches and third the apotheosis of the soldier turned literary chronicler, whose survival constitutes his 'victory'. This three part theme can also be described in terms of preparation, execution and finally critique.

Although this narrative is styled on the so-called 'disillusionment texts' like *Memoirs of an Infantry Officer, Undertones of War* and *Goodbye to All That*, it has an added dimension.[7] It is a reminder of the strong colonial ties of that time. For some readers it may come as a surprise to find that not only did colonials serve with Dominion forces, in many cases they also paid their own passage to England. It would have been inconceivable to them that South Africans would one day be forbidden to set foot on British soil without first obtaining a visa—while other Commonwealth citizens can travel freely. In the age of steamships, migration throughout the Empire was relatively easy. The Reid family had a presence in Canada for twenty five years. Harry lived in South Africa all his adult life. His military service extended from the 1914 South African Rebellion, through German South West Africa, France and Flanders to the Rand Revolt of 1922.

After the First World War, it was usually former military officers who were appointed to record the regimental histories—and the results were generally 'militaristic'. The official history of the 7th Royal Inniskilling Fusiliers was brought out in 1920 by G. A. Cooper Walker, who as a lieutenant, served alongside the Reid brothers. I have made liberal use of his work *The Book of the Seventh Service Battalion, The Royal Inniskilling Fusiliers from Tipperary to Ypres* in order to ascertain dates, names and significant events in the history of the battalion.[8]

Contrary to a commonly-held belief, poems cannot always stand irrespective of context. In *Deveron to Devastation,* A. D. Reid's work is given context by providing some background and filling in the gaps. Just as Anthony Boden used an articulation of biography to introduce the poetry of F. W. Harvey, I have placed A. D. Reid's verse and prose within the life of the battalion.[9] As a framework, I was fortunate to have the unpublished memoirs of Alex's brother, H. F. (Harry) Reid, who was the transport officer in the same battalion. Harry had neither his brother's classical education nor his talent for the written word, and for the most part, his narrative has been paraphrased. In the postmodernist fashion, I have used some empathy and intuition, but the extracts from Alex's journal are reproduced verbatim.

Although his classical education shows in his vocabulary, Alex does not make use of the metaphor and symbolism, but I do not make any attempt at literary criticism. The literary merits of A. D. Reid's poems are not being judged. His work should be seen as a 'human document'—all the more powerful and moving because it comes from a long cultural tradition. The soldier-poet was a romantic figure, upholder of moral values, truth-teller *par excellence,* 'who faced fear and death and spoke about them to the yet unknowing world.'[10]

Years of writing reports for his superiors would have curbed any tendency towards 'flowery' prose, and being a professional soldier, Reid wrote nothing that can be considered pacifistic, angry nor passionate. A young subaltern fresh out of school would be better equipped for that. Good or bad, his 'request' has added significance given the fact that he was destined 'to vanish as earthly clay'. It is the best that you, the reader, be the judge. Here is a sample:

A Request

You may bury me up on a mountain crest,
By the trail of the mist and the eagle's nest.
On some wild crag might my carcass rest,
Where the foot of man scarce trod.
Or bury me deep where a sapling grows,
Its quality rare from my rotting bones.
As it strikes its roots in the earth and stones,

And watches the seasons nod.
Or, oh to be buried in a cavern dim,
Where ghostly fish in green pools swim!
My spirit would haunt the ocean's brim,
As the tale of the world went by.
And yet I'd be buried where the four roads meet,
Or where the worm's food thrums to the traffic's beat.
And the echo, echo of hurrying feet,
As they backwards and forwards fly.
But no, I'll be buried far out at sea,
Now the ship is stopped and my corpse shoots free.
In a shotted shroud what once was me,
Is afloat in the middle way.
In life, great space is my heart's desire,
To the places free, my thoughts aspire.
So my body may go to the cleansing fire,
But not to a crowded bay.
But bury me not with a drear black hearse,
Black string of cabs and a generous purse.
I do not consider the wild ways worse,
To vanish as earthly clay.
Nor let my friends put on the black,
Nor mourn long days for the one they lack.
But tune their heartstrings to sound a crack,
Of cheer for the spirit free.
And when they meet let them talk and nod,
'we knew his faults and the ways he trod'.
There was much of the brute and a mite of God,
But now of the brute he is free.
So bury it low or bury it high,
The body dross where'er it lie.
And do not mourn for the things that die,
But shout for the spirit free.

A leading oral historian, Alistair Thomson, conducted extensive interviews while researching Australian memories of the First World War, the popular legend of 'Anzac' (Australia and New Zealand Corps) and the relationship between individual memories and national legend. Thomson's research shows how some memories are highlighted while others are repressed and silenced. Soldiering men dominated the family mythology of his childhood. His great-uncle, Boyd Thomson, was a promising architect and a poet. Following his death on the Somme in 1916, his memory became a romantic tradition in the family, upholding the values of his school, his social class and the duty of service for the nation. He represented a talent never allowed to mature. By contrast, Alistair Thomson's own grandfather, Hector, was seldom mentioned even though he earned the Military Medal for bravery. Life for him was hard, exacerbated by the Great Depression and ill health.[11] Clearly, this was a recurring theme of the day, and one which presents itself again here.

The way in which the war is remembered has long been an area of academic research, and as modern historiography has shown, memory is a highly subjective construction of experience. This is partly as a result of what G. L. Mosse refers to as 'The myth of the war experience'. It refers to a whole series of attitudes which helped men confront and accept what had previously been beyond the realm of human experience, but it could not eliminate memories of the past. Veterans tried to forget the horrors as quickly as possible but remembered the companionship, purposefulness and the security of the war.[12]

Inherent in the myth of the war experience is 'The cult of the fallen soldier' which in turn is kept alive by pilgrimages to the battlefields, bleak monuments and idyllic war cemeteries, as well as the literature which began to proliferate a decade after the war had ended. This literature, together with the needs of the post-war society, distorted the collective memory. Perhaps now, through the prism of the past century, the lives of the two brother officers will take on a different perspective.

CHAPTER 1

Map reference:
J. 7. B. 70. 05

Death favoured me from the first, well knowing I could not endure
To wait on him day by day. He quitted my betters and came
Whistling over the fields, and when he had made all sure,
'Thyne line is at an end,' he said, 'but at least I have saved its name.'
Rudyard Kipling—from *Epitaphs of the War*

Third Ypres, otherwise known as the Battle of Passchendaele, began at ten minutes to four on the morning of 31 July 1917. By ten o'clock, Colonel Alex Reid was dead and the assault had ground to a halt. At a transport camp four miles to the rear, Lieutenant Harry Reid was given the shocking news. His commanding officer, who could also be called a friend, darkened the doorway and blurted out, 'Your brother was killed this morning during the attack.'

It had been only three weeks since Alex had been reassigned from his regimental fraternity to take command of the 1st Royal Irish Rifles—a battalion made up of strangers and replacements thrown together to share the same fate. Up until his transfer on promotion, Alex had been second in command of the 7th Royal Inniskilling Fusiliers, and he was one of its founding fathers. His younger brother, Harry, was the transport officer within the same close-knit family.

Accustomed to first reports being little more than wild rumours, Harry at first held on to the hope that the information was incorrect. But the fact remained, his brother had been sent to fill a dead man's shoes and now he too had been killed in what was being called a 'dud show'. To the men he was with at the time, Alex was just another nameless officer intent on leading them to their deaths, and none were likely to care if his corpse should turn to dross where it lay. Accordingly, Harry resolved to find his brother and have him buried among friends at Philosophe near

Loos, where Alex himself had been instrumental in the establishment of a regimental cemetery, together with a memorial fund to ensure its upkeep.

Behind the lines, between the villages of Vlamertinghe and Poperinghe, the frenetic activity gave the impression of an anthill which had been disturbed, but as his brigade was in reserve Harry was allowed the opportunity to search the battlefield for his brother and he instructed his groom to be ready with his horse before dawn the next day. With a heavy heart, under a leaden sky, Harry set off for the HQ of the 25th Brigade which was situated at Hooge, about four miles east of Ypres. The experiences of that day would become embedded in Harry's being, and recorded in his memoirs in a chapter with the heading 'J. 7. B. 70. 05'—the map reference of the exact spot where Alex's body lay:

It had been raining hard for some time and the roads were inundated. As we splashed our way along, our progress was impeded by floating logs and debris of all kinds. I had not gone very far when I fell in with a colonel of a regiment, the name of which I have forgotten, who was riding in my direction. I told him that I was going to the 8th Divisional front to endeavour to find my brother's body and bring it down from the line. The colonel invited me to his battalion HQ which was nearby. After some tea, he offered to have a sergeant and six men accompany me. Naturally, I did not refuse an offer made with such consideration and kindness and I started off with the men he had placed at my disposal. To ride over the shell and rain-soaked ground was impossible, so I sent my groom back to camp with my horse. In any case, I preferred to walk with the sergeant and the men of my party.

The road we traversed was the main artery of the battlefield which went from Ypres in the direction of Menin. The surface had been destroyed by almost continuous shell fire over a period of several weeks. A crossroads given the name of 'Hellfire Corner' was a particularly unpleasant spot, and we were fortunate in passing it at a time of comparative quiet. At length, we arrived at Hooge, where the Brigade HQ was housed. Behind a screen wall, I found some steps leading down into the brigadier's concrete bunker. He received me in a pleasant and friendly manner but did not think that I had very much chance of success and said that I was more likely to become a casualty myself as the Germans were now counter-attacking. Also, he told me that the advance on the whole 5th Army front had been held up owing to lack of artillery support and weather conditions. My response was, 'I have started out on my expedition and I wish to continue'. The brigadier thereupon gave me the location to which the Royal Irish Rifles, Alex's regiment, had been withdrawn after suffering heavy casualties.

On coming up from the brigadier's bunker, I surveyed the terrain. A small lake lay to the north in front of me called Bellewaarde Lake. It had at one time been surrounded by trees, now only a few shattered stumps remained. The land around it, as far as one could see, had been churned by shell fire and reduced to a complete swamp by the continuous rain. It occurred to me that it would be almost impossible to bring Alex's body back to the road even if I found him, yet I felt that I could not subject the sergeant and his men to the fatigue and risk of attempting such a task, particularly as they did not belong to my regiment. I therefore gave the sergeant a message of thanks to his colonel and I requested him to take his men back to his unit.

I continued on my way and came to the HQ of the 1st Royal Irish Rifles. The battalion had suffered severely and the remaining officers had hardly had time to recover from their experiences of the preceding night. The officer in charge, [probably Captain Whitfield], informed me of how Alex had met his death. Apparently, on reaching Westhoek, the progress of the battalion was held up and Alex went ahead to ascertain the position. He was killed almost instantly by machine gun fire. I was told that an attempt had been made to bring his body back but was abandoned owing to the rapid advance of the enemy behind a barrage of shell fire. No offer of a guide to accompany me was forthcoming—not surprisingly since that location was now in no man's land and under the control of the enemy. [There is no such place as Westhoek in the Zonnebeke area today. It existed only on the trench maps of the time.]

I was given a map spotting of the place where the ill-fated action took place, namely J. 7. B. 70. 05, and armed with this information, continued towards the existing front line. The condition of the shell-torn ground is known only to those who saw it with their own eyes, for it cannot be described in words. At times, it was hardly possible to obtain a firm foothold round the edges of the shell holes full of mud and water. However, I continued until I came to a line of trenches held by the Cheshire Regiment. This was the front line and according to my map, Alex's body was lying at Jabber Trench somewhere ahead. There was some enemy fire but things seemed to have quietened down. Here I stayed for a while, hoping to get some information, but as the Cheshires had only recently taken over their position and were somewhat preoccupied, I came to the conclusion that there was no point in remaining there and I went on alone.

The day was passing and I had to concede that my cause was a hopeless one, thus I took the grim decision to give up the attempt. Soon I realized that it was not going to be easy to get back to the Menin road. The sun was setting and the mist was beginning to rise from the slimy mass which encompassed me from every side. If I stood still, my feet sank into the swamp, and continually pulling them out before taking another step began to tell on my strength. I had been on the move since dawn and had not thought of providing myself with any food. My feet began to sink deeper and deeper with every step, I needed to rest and I sank down on a log half buried in the mud. After resting a few seconds, I discovered that I was sitting not on the trunk of a tree but on the trunk of a dead body. Quickly, I got on my feet and continued my struggle.

The sun had now set and the light was fading out of the sky. The mist thickened. With the mud up to my knees, the effort to release each leg felt as if my entrails were being sucked out of my body. I stumbled against a shattered tree stump and leaned against it for a moment. A queer feeling made me turn my head and I found I was leaning against a mud-covered headless corpse. The protruding spine gave the impression of a shattered tree stump. Immediately, I staggered on. Death had held no terror now, it was only the act of dying, which I considered to be like having a tooth pulled, just a sudden pang and then relief.

The mist had closed in upon me. I could not see more than two or three yards. Soon I became fixed in the thick mud, gradually sinking up to my waist. Further progress was impossible. Exhausted, my body fell over in the malodorous mud, I simply could not keep myself upright. The smell of death was around me and I welcomed the thought of lying in some soft, moist earth. As the darkness enveloped me, I felt a delightful sensation of peacefulness. This shell hole was my grave and it felt right and proper. My family and friends seemed in a misty past. I longed to let go, but fleetingly, I thought of my mother. Losing her beloved Alex would be hard enough for her to bear. I simply had to hang on for her sake.

My face was now half immersed in the mud, but in the distance I thought I heard two men talking. Was it a delusion? I raised my head and shouted. The noise seemed to stop—as though they were listening. I shouted again. The talking resumed and seemed to be nearer, again I shouted. Suddenly, two figures appeared out of the mist beside me. They were stretcher bearers returning from the line. Together, they hauled me out, and one on each side, supported me to the road. I was placed in an ambulance, labelled 'found exhausted in no man's land' and taken to a casualty clearing station.

The next day, Harry returned to his camp mortified by his failure. It took only two days for Margaret Reid to receive the telegram informing her that her son was 'missing, presumed killed'. Despite the testimony of those who saw him fall, an element of hope and uncertainty remained. Anguish and anxiety would from now on be her lot in life—the joy had been snuffed out.

As his regiment was not yet engaged in the fighting, Harry was able to go over to the headquarters of the 1st Royal Irish Rifles to pack up Alex's personal effects and prepare them for shipping to Canada. It was on this occasion that he had first sight of the field service book which Alex had used as a diary. Wanting to satisfy himself that there was nothing in it which their mother would find distressing, he sat down on Alex's valise to read. It commenced thus:

Diary of A. D. Reid: To be forwarded to Mrs M. Reid, Cowichan Station, Vancouver Island.

Opened on: 9/4/1916

Closed on:_____

Suddenly ten minutes ago, I decided to keep a diary, and in case the resolution should cool rushed off to get a book from the orderly room. I have kept a diary before, so that I know perfectly well what I am undertaking. As a matter of fact, a diary is an infernal nuisance. Personally, I prefer to revert to memory for anything that is really worth remembering, and when you come to consider a day's happenings, there is not much. The rest can go on forever as far as I'm concerned. How I imagine peoples' ideas vary considerably as to what is worth remembering, something to the memory of some day of extra ordinary jollity, others the requisition of their hearts love, a day's report, a journey and so on. A diarist may keep an accurate second of dates, events, names of often pleased information. Let them all go, say I. What does a date matter? What is it that such and such a day was fine, or that heaviest fall of snow, the wettest summer occurred in such year. This is a very wrong attitude, I know. The collection of false information is valuable for categorizing of facts and furtherance of human knowledge. Quite so, but I am only speaking for myself. My position is unassailable. I please only myself. Therefore although I keep a diary, it is some form of habit and to mark the march of life. As far as I know, time as we know it does not exist, except as experienced on earth. One must accommodate oneself more or less to ones surroundings.

The real milestones are much more indefinite than can be nailed down by a date. They are the beginnings of a new epoch in one's life where one grasps more thought with greater completeness and more vividly than one has ever done. This thought has at odd times flitted through one's mind, at first with considerable interval of time between each becoming gradually more frequent but more elusive just as a bird darting into a room flutters in a movement round the hand stretched to catch it and is gone. A day comes when in a blaze of insight the thought stretches clear across one's mind. In that movement one grasps it in its entirety and the new knowledge is at last one's for always.

CHAPTER 2

To the Corners of the Empire

Six foot three inches tall, with the build of a rugby football player, William Thomas Reid cut a fine figure in his Highlander regalia, towering above his fellow officers on parade. Being an officer in the 3rd Battalion (militia) Gordon Highlanders was just a hobby for William, but he attained the rank of captain and was appointed Justice of the Peace. His maternal grandmother was the one with the necessary pedigree for his advancement since she was the daughter of Colonel Thomas Gordon of the Castle of Park. It was asserted in William's obituary that he was a conservative in politics 'greatly esteemed by his tenantry as a liberal and generous landlord'.

In the typical Victorian way, William and his wife Margaret remained aloof from their children, leaving them in the care of a governess at every opportunity. Rachel was the oldest but the son and heir was Alexander Daniel (Alex), born in 1882. Henry Francis (Harry) was the youngest child, quite sickly, and by his own admission, spoiled and overly protected by his mother. 'What Harry wanted Harry got' Rachel would say. There was another brother, Stewart, a year younger than Alex, but his existence was purposefully erased from his family's memory. Genealogical research revealed only that his occupation was 'soldier' and he died in the Springfield Mental Hospital in Tooting aged 54.

The family home was at Hazelwood on the outskirts of Dufftown, in Banffshire, but William spent most of his time with his mistress in their London love nest and when he was in Scotland, he preferred to stay on his hunting estate, Ardmeallie, supervising the large staff and entertaining the sportsmen and their entourages who had come up from London by overnight train. Ardmeallie lies astride the River Deveron in the heartland of the Duff Gordons. The Old Marnoch kirkyard is part of the estate.

During one of his visits to Ardmeallie, William caught a chill from which he never recovered. He was 41 years old with a strong constitution, so his death was a shock, especially when it was found that there was another woman's name engraved on the inside of his wedding band, but even more devastating was the discovery that his estate was insolvent. It was 1899 and Alex was completing his last year of school prior to entering the Royal Military College at Sandhurst. Harry was thirteen and on the threshold of entering some or other prestigious public school but now his hopes of being groomed as a gentleman were dashed.

Alex was educated at Westminster School, one of the oldest and most prestigious institutions in all England. The buildings exude history and are practically impregnated with the public school spirit. Westminster Abbey is in fact the school chapel. Public school boys at the turn of the century wore flannel trousers, butterfly collars and jackets slit up the back. A sort of caste system prevailed, marked by distinctions in dress. No friendship could exist between boys of different houses or different ages—even if they were next-door neighbours at home. Because his father had a residence at 5 West Cromwell Road, Kensington, Alex was in the Home Boarder's House. The emphasis was on sport and character training, but it was also expected of pupils to be able to conjugate verbs in Latin and Greek—not to mention French.

Westminster School sent forth many young men rightly trained in body, mind and character. Entry to Sandhurst was almost guaranteed. It was a breeding ground of future Prime Ministers, and six former pupils won the Victoria Cross—two of them in the Great War. Arthur Martin-Leake, a medical doctor, was the first of only three people in history to have won the VC twice. The first time was at Vlakfontein during the Anglo-Boer War—for his work tending the wounded under fire. Another Old Westminster to win the VC in the Great War was Lieutenant-Colonel William Clark-Kennedy who had much in common with Alex, being Scottish by birth and Canadian by adoption.

Once his training as a Gentleman Cadet at the Royal Military College was completed, Alex's commission was gazetted in July 1900 as a second lieutenant with a view to an appointment to the Indian Staff Corps. In his class were a number of 'Queens India Cadets'—boys whose fathers had served the crown while stationed in India. European personnel were recruited to staff Indian regiments and since officers were obliged to pay out of their own pockets for expenses such as uniforms, laundry bills and mess fees, India offered a cheaper option. It appears from the Westminster School records that Alex was first attached to the Black Watch, and other scraps of information suggest that he was then posted to the 52nd Sikhs (Frontier Force).

Before being posted to their Indian Army regiments, new officers were first given a period of orientation where subalterns were taught that in certain regiments, talking 'shop' in the mess was taboo. A subaltern who was caught reading a military book in the mess was told to 'get out'. Lessons in etiquette revealed that gentlemen did not smoke pipes in the ante-room but could do so in the billiard room. Furthermore, no subaltern could leave the mess until every other guest had left. The training was distinctly 'last century' where the battalion was taught to advance in tight bunches of about twenty men and for the final assault, they would form a straight line, dressed to the right and walk forward cheering as they went.

Over a period of fifty years, the Indian Army had been undertaking small wars and expeditions against the Pathan tribes on the Northwest Frontier, but by 1897 they had finally been crushed. It was a time of relative peace for the British Empire everywhere, and although promotion was slow, life was good in the Indian Army. The work of the Staff Corps or General Staff was nice and 'cushy' (the word itself comes from the time of the Raj). Furlough was usually generously granted to allow officers the opportunity to find themselves a wife.

One often gets the impression that leisure time was spent in an idyllic round of shooting, dances, polo and picnics. However, it was not an ideal life for families. Children over the age of six were invariably sent back to England for their schooling and would seldom see their parents during the next ten years. During the school holidays, they would be farmed out to relatives or lodged with paid guardians. There was a shortage of eligible women in India and mixing between the races was unacceptable. In the sweltering summer months, English families would migrate to the hill stations where the altitude provided some relief from the humidity. Typically, the husbands remained at their posts, toiling away on the hot plains, and only joined their families on the odd occasion. Gossip maintained that these hill stations were a hotbed of marital intrigue. Perhaps the misty mountains made the ladies lose their inhibitions and think with fervour of romps on tiger skin divans.

In the realm of historic events, the highpoint of Alex's posting was the occasion of a visit by the Prince and Princess of Wales. On 8 December 1905, at Rawalpindi, there was an impressive parade and march-past of almost every regiment in the Indian Army under command of Horatio Herbert Viscount Kitchener, commander-in-chief in India. It was the social event of the decade and a most colourful spectacle. More than fifty years had passed since the Indian Mutiny of 1857 but the British army still had an uneasy relationship with the local population. In a way, it was a society under siege.

School boys were fed a healthy diet of Rudyard Kipling, and his call for Empire builders by way of his *White Man's Burden* resulted in many young men like Harry deciding to head for the colonies. Through some sort of synchronicity, his path was to follow Kipling all the way to Cape Town and Vancouver. On being awarded the Nobel Prize for Literature in 1907, Kipling was at the height of his career but Harry was at a loose end with no profession or prospects. India held its attractions. Even middle class administrators were treated like Sahibs. Anglo-Indians were pampered and pretentious. On remote tea plantations, it was not unusual for a husband and wife living on their own to change into evening dress for supper. 'One must keep up standards, not let oneself go native.'

In 1907, at Alex's invitation, Harry set off for India, sailing via Cape Town. Travelling first class was ideal for establishing social connections, and his investment paid off. On board the mail steamer, he was introduced to a wealthy businessman named Harry Mosenthal who was a director of the De Beers diamond mining company and a shareholder in various gold mining operations, including Rand Mines. He moved in high circles in Europe and South Africa and was a close friend of the Rothschild family, Cecil Rhodes and many of the other 'Rand Lords'. Counted among his friends and colleagues were Barney Barnato, Charles Rudd, Ernest Oppenheimer, Leander Starr Jameson and Sir Donald Currie—the founder of the Union Castle shipping line but better known for the Curry Cup which he contributed to South African rugby.

Mosenthal Brothers was one of the oldest and most established mercantile houses in South Africa. Since the firm had started off as an importer and exporter of goods, the head office had been established in Port Elizabeth which was at the time South Africa's second biggest city. The Eastern Cape hinterland produced citrus fruit, wool and ostrich feathers. When mining became the company's main interest, offices were opened in Johannesburg, Kimberley and Pretoria. Besides their South African mining interests, the Mosenthals were involved in copper mining in Australia and America and trade in Bechuanaland and Rhodesia.

Harry Mosenthal was a short, debonair man sporting a *pince-nez*. Although a trifle portly, he had once played cricket for the Transvaal against Kimberley and was a great sports supporter. While he had an office and a home in London, he spent much of his time in South Africa. On his journeys to and fro, he usually travelled with his diminutive wife Johanna and a number of employees—including the butler and the maid.

With their distinctive lavender-coloured hulls and red funnels topped in black, the Union-Castle Line had one ship leaving Southampton and another leaving Cape Town every Thursday at 4.00 p.m. While at sea, during the day, there were concerts and games on deck, and in the evenings, elegantly dressed ladies and gentlemen would dance to the traditional waltzes, marches and polkas. The scandalous tango only hit Europe in 1913, and the ragtime fad had also not yet made its appearance. After a dinner of roast rib of beef with potatoes château in the first class dining room, the men gathered in the smoking room. Over port and cigars, the conversation invariably turned to the business of mining. One such evening, Harry Mosenthal talked his namesake into making South Africa his new home, offering him a job as his private secretary.

From the very day that Harry set foot in South Africa, mining labour was in a state of turmoil, taking the form of strikes of varying severity, but in 1913 the troubles on the Witwatersrand were especially serious. It was a precursor of the cataclysm to come. Imperial troops were rushed into the centre of Johannesburg to help the police put a stop to looting and to break up a massive meeting. Strikers hunted down mine bosses in the Rand Club but were held back by the troops. A miner, Labuschagne, bared his chest and defiantly cried 'Shoot!' The soldiers obliged and Labuschagne sank to the ground, dead. An unsatisfactory peace resulted from a conference at the Carlton Hotel, but J. C. Smuts, the Prime Minister was smarting. Smuts summarily deported the nine leaders, none of whom were born in the country. On future occasions his response would be more heavy-handed.

Politically, the new Union was in a state of disunity but it was the policy of Mosenthal Brothers not to become involved in politics. During the Boer War they had suffered financial losses yet by 1913 had recovered sufficiently to build a new store in Johannesburg at 91 Market Street. It was a solid eight storey building with slow, clanking, wrought iron lifts and a long mahogany counter. At that time, very little was manufactured in South Africa and Mosenthal Brothers had the agencies to supply products ranging from dynamite, to Nestlé condensed milk and Schweppes mineral waters.

Alex's career with the Indian Army staff corps spanned from 1902 to his retirement in 1909. Although seven years was standard, there was no obligatory period of service since a cadet's family paid for his education at Sandhurst. Without the patronage of a senior officer to help him get on, and no opportunity to perform an act of death defying valour, Lieutenant A. D. Reid's prospects of promotion were poor. England had nothing to offer a retired Indian Army officer without independent wealth, and besides, great space was his heart's desire. It seems that anyone who had spent time in India felt something akin to bereavement when they retired to England. They longed for the spectacular sunsets, the chattering monkeys and the squawking of the parrots in the garden.

For some years now, the attractions of British Colombia and Vancouver Island in particular had been a favourite topic of conversation in drawing rooms throughout the empire. In books, magazines, letters, and by word of mouth, visitors and residents advertised this land of sunshine and sea breezes. It seemed to be the destination of choice for soldiers, sailors and civil servants who manned and protected the British Empire. Journalists and world travellers described Victoria Island as being unrivalled in its beauty and benign climate. One visitor compared it to Honolulu—but without the monotonous climate. Vancouver also attracted 'refugees' from the rest of Canada wanting to escape the freezing winters and the baking summers. The island was virtually free of the mosquitoes and flies which plagued the interior.

Like a cholera epidemic, news had gone around in India that Vancouver was the best place in the world for a retired Indian Army man. After settling there, officers from the same regiments still kept in touch and Alex's former colleagues described the greenness of the land, freshened by the delicate rain—not unlike the mountainous parts of Ceylon and Kashmir. Newspapers in India told of unrivalled hunting and fishing in an article entitled 'A sportsman's Eden'. This would have held great appeal for Alex. Moreover, Vancouver Island was seen as a Shangri-la, a haven from life in the outside world. Just prior to the outbreak of war, *The Times of India Illustrated Weekly* reinforced the island's reputation as 'a home for the Anglo-Indian'.

Having lost Hazelwood, her home in Dufftown, Alex's mother would not have needed much convincing to join him in Canada, bringing Rachel and Stewart with her. In 1909, British Columbia was booming and the Cowichan Valley had a thriving community of Anglo-Indians. The mining and timber industries were taking off. Wealthier residents of the city of Victoria had country homes on the various lakes. For the genteel English, it was home from home. It even rained as in the mother country—starting with a moist feeling in the air and developing into a thorough soaking. In the city, the upper classes had their Chinese servants, invitations to dances, tennis parties and the theatre. The countryside produced what was needed without sacrificing beauty for utility. There could have been no more agreeable society with so much of the English tradition and sentiment.

The completion of the Canadian Pacific Railway (CPR) in 1886 had the effect of opening up the west coast. In fact, the CPR ran its own fleet of ships, operated by the Canadian Pacific Steamship Company. Perhaps the company is best remembered for the *Empress of Ireland*, which after a collision, went down in the St Lawrence River with the loss of more than a thousand souls. During the war, the CPR put its entire travel system of railways, ships, hotels, shops and telegraphs at the disposal of the British Empire. Fifty two of the company's ships were pressed into service, carrying more than a million troops and passengers and four million tons of cargo—many were sunk.

Vancouver Island at the time was inhabited with more than its fair share of eccentric characters, including white hunters from Africa, failed coffee farmers from Ceylon, minor noblemen and assorted adventurers. But it was the ex-army types who predominated—giving rise to the British Imperial Campaigner's Association (BICA) which was founded in 1908 and consisted mainly of Boer War and Indian Army veterans. Another society which was founded only a year before Margaret Reid's death in 1934, and three years before the death of the great man himself, was the Kipling Society. The 'Kipling Effect' was pervasive in this valley since Kipling had visited there in 1907.

Sir H. Rider Haggard epitomized the type of Victorian adventurer who voyaged between England, Southern Africa and British Colombia. Rider Haggard was the author of *King Solomon's Mines*, *She* and many other books featuring the character Alan Quartermain—said to have been based on the real life hunter-explorer, Frederick Courtenay Selous. Rider Haggard's older brother, Andrew, retired to the Cowichan Valley in 1907. Here he hunted and fished and wrote more than two dozen books of poetry, historical fiction and popular history. These did not however win him a fraction of the fame which his younger brother enjoyed. Rider Haggard had a home in South Africa but he had once thought of moving to Vancouver Island and may have regretted his decision not to do so as he considered it to be one of the most beautiful places on earth.

In June 1911, a Canadian census worker found Margaret Reid and two of her children, Rachel and Stewart, at Lake Shawnigan, but Alex was not with them at that time. If he was not at home in Cowichan Station, perhaps he had gone fishing or was away on business. At the height of its fortunes in 1913, the settlement of Cowichan Station consisted of two general stores, two estate agents, a hardware store, butcher shop, two Chinese laundries, a smithy, shoemaker, doctor, two boarding houses and two churches.

The valley had a preponderance of Anglicans, and St Andrews Church was the focal point of the community. Margaret devoted her life to the parish and gardened assiduously. On her death in 1934, she was buried in the churchyard and Rachel, still a spinster, emigrated to South Africa where she lived out the rest of her days in Durban.

Having been asked for increasing monetary assistance, Harry correctly assumed that his brother's farming venture was not a success. Land was cheap and opportunities were plentiful but like many before him—and since—he underestimated the challenges of poultry farming. As his situation deteriorated, Alex expressed a desire to leave British Colombia, so when the war came along it relieved him of further anxiety. As he was still on the reserve, he was called up automatically when the regular army mobilized.

CHAPTER 3

'War' in German
South West Africa

Like everyone else, Harry was swept up in a tide of emotion when war was declared in August 1914. For 'home-born' men, the call was especially strong, partly out of patriotism, partly a feeling that one ought not to be left out of it when others went. While some immediately set off to join British regiments, paying their own passage, Harry decided to join a regiment which was by tradition, a Johannesburg unit. The Imperial Light Horse (ILH) had a proud reputation originating from the Boer War, and he was happy to serve in the 1st ILH with the rank of trooper—at the mature age of 28. Many wealthy farmers, professional men and even former officers of the Anglo-Boer War enlisted as troopers rather than be left out.

One of the outstanding personalities who enlisted as a trooper in the ILH in the South West Africa campaign was Stanley Harris who became a Lieutenant-Colonel in the British Army during the 1939-45 war. Wounded at the battle of the Somme while serving with the Royal Field Artillery, he took up ballroom dancing to aid his convalescence. A year later, he won the waltz section of the world ballroom dancing championships. Having recovered from his wounds, he later had the distinction of playing rugby internationals for England, South Africa and the British Lions. This all-rounder of all time then played water polo for England and won Springbok colours for boxing and tennis.

After a short period of training at Booysens Camp and at the Milner Park show grounds, the regiment entrained for Cape Town where the ILH camp was situated on Cecil Rhodes' Estate at Rondebosch—the magnificent Groote Schuur. Although well received by the local population, some residents of Muizenberg may have been shocked by the sight of a squadron of 130 naked men bathing with their horses in the surf. The horses seemed to enjoy the water.

South Africa's participation in the war coincided with another national calamity—the outbreak of the 1914 Rebellion. A large section of the population on the *platteland* (country districts) was anti-British and sympathetic to the German cause. The rebel cause was given impetus by the prophet, Nicolaas 'Siener' van Rensburg. 'Siener' (meaning 'seer') had a vision of fighting bulls and his interpretation was that Germany would win the war. Approximately 12,000 Boers formed themselves into commandos and took to the field.

The government considered the rebellion to be a Boer squabble and wanted to keep it in the family. Citizen Force regiments were kept out of the fray but the Transvaal Scottish and newly formed South African Irish were deployed to protect Pretoria. While one squadron of the ILH had already landed at Luderitzbucht, another small contingent was sent by train to the Northern Cape to prevent the rebel leader, Manie Maritz, with his 600 men, from linking up with the German forces across the border. One by one, the rebel bands were cornered and forced to surrender. All were given amnesty except for one, Jopie Fourie, who was executed because he was a member of the military and had crossed over to the rebels, uniform and all. All this passed almost unnoticed in the outside world but the divisions existed in South Africa for many years to come.

South West Africa is a vast, arid territory of over 317,000 square miles and was defended by about 8,000 German troops. South African forces invaded from the south and at two points along the coast. The ILH was split among the three columns, the 2nd ILH landed at Luderitzbucht as part of the Central Force. The horses were slung over the side and allowed to swim to shore. Some of the overfed and under-exercised horses disappeared into the interior—thus adding to the gene pool of the wild horses which still roam the desert.

While Harry was still doing his training in Johannesburg with the rest of the 1st ILH, one squadron ('D' Squadron) had already been attached to the small force which had landed at Luderitzbucht on 18 September. The town had been deserted and they fought their first action on 26 September 1914 at Kolmanskop just inland from Luderitzbucht while trying to intercept the German retreat. Four members of the regiment were killed in this skirmish—two of them brothers. Rex and Wilfred Winslow were both top tennis players and had been schooled at St John's College in Johannesburg. Rex was hit first in the chest. Wilfred ran across to help his brother and was shot through the neck while trying to give him water. The German who did the shooting then surrendered. Reverend Eustace Hill, who was to become a legendary figure on the Western Front, read the first of many funeral services that he would have to conduct. He had been their school chaplain and knew the boys well. The whole brigade was present.

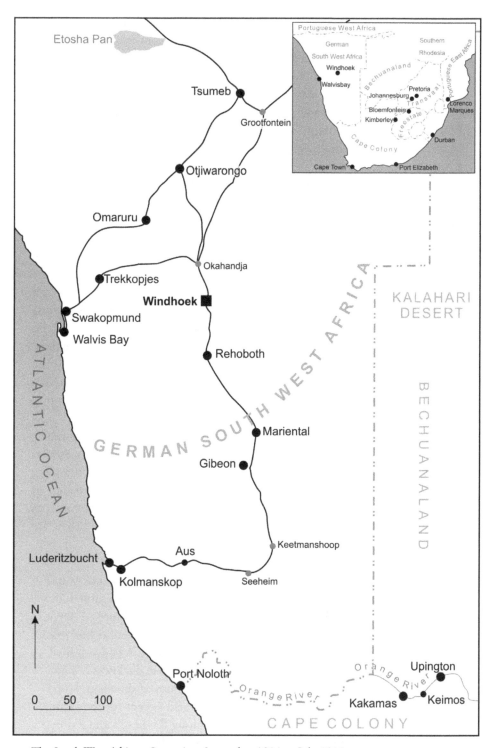

The South West African Campaign, September 1914 to July 1915.

The brothers were buried in one grave and someone painted a wooden plaque which read: 'Tell England, ye who pass this monument, that we who lie here, serving her, died content.' In what is now called 'the spirit of 1914', this was a not uncommon sentiment.

It was on Christmas day that the 1st ILH (minus 'D' Squadron at Luderitzbucht) sailed into Walvisbay as part of the Northern Expeditionary Force. This time the horses were lowered with slings onto rafts (40 horses or mules to a raft) which were then towed through the surf by men in the water. Once again, a bunch of spooked horses broke free and galloped into the dunes. The Germans sent a note thanking the South Africans for the remounts. As a cavalryman, Harry became proficient at manhandling obstinate horses, mules and even some captured camels up and down sand dunes and on and off trains using railway sleepers as steps. The experience would hold him in good stead for his role as a transport officer in France and Flanders.

Late one afternoon, eighteen days after disembarking at Walvisbay, a 350 strong reconnaissance force under Colonel P. C. B. Skinner set out for Swakopmund, 23 miles up the coast. The column which included the ILH, Grobbelaar's Scouts and a machine gun detachment rode in the dark along the shoreline. Having ploughed through the soft sand for some miles along the beach, Harry's squadron, which formed the rear guard, halted and Cossack posts were sent forward to take up positions among the sand dunes.

A Cossack post, being a single outpost as opposed to a line of sentinels, comprised one NCO and three men. The dunes varied in height up to two or three hundred feet and stretched towards Swakopmund and inland as far as the eye could see—a dun coloured world of silence with no sign of animal or human life. As the main party continued the advance towards Swakopmund, Harry sat atop his sand dune and was inspired to write lyrical prose:

> We drew lots and each trooper took two hours on and two hours off. I drew first guard and climbed to the summit of the designated sand dune. The sun had set but a short period of twilight remained. I looked down on the beach and beyond across the South Atlantic to the far horizon. The sea was calm and a saffron sky glowed where the sun had vanished, changing as I looked to palest emerald. Then at once darkness fell and the brightness of the stars contrasted with blackness of the night. Not a sound could be heard in this strange silent world except for the gentle whisper of tiny waves as they rose and fell along the beach and a quiet murmur as light breezes stirred the sand upon the dunes.

Around dawn, the silence was shattered by the sound of detonating mines which had been planted by the retreating Germans. Two troops of 'B' squadron had taken a turn to the right and ploughed across the sand dunes to enter the town from the east but were too late to cut off the retreating enemy. Fortunately the mines caused no serious damage. The Germans withdrew to the outskirts of Swakopmund and the South African troops remained in the town for many weeks, bored to tears. Nevertheless, after the bleakness of Walvisbay, Swakopmund was a veritable holiday resort with hotels, beer gardens and music halls.

Just outside Swakopmund, the ILH maintained a Cossack post during the day-time. One morning, on arriving at the top of their designated dune, some troopers found a note held down by a bottle of beer asking for cigarettes in exchange. Trading with the enemy continued for some time, thereby earning a new moniker for the ILH—Ilicit Liquor Hunters.

The only real action involving the Northern Force in the campaign took place at Trekkoppies. With the support of artillery, the Germans attacked resolutely and got to within 300 yards of the Kimberley Regiments' trenches but some armoured cars (thought by the Germans to be water carts) opened up a deadly fire. The ILH was kept in reserve, waiting to counter attack but took no major part, and came in for some adverse criticism. The death toll was eleven Germans and nine South Africans, one of whom was Signaller G. S. Reid aged 62 years.

Windhoek, the capital, was found to be a clean and modern town with imposing administrative buildings. It was given up without a shot being fired and the conquering army of shaggy Boers and soldiers in tattered khaki paraded proudly in the main square. Three hundred hungry and nervous civilians had stayed behind. At first, there was a bit of looting which resulted in strict orders that there was to be no looting of food. The local paper, the *Sudwest*, was complimentary of the South African troops and life in the town soon reverted to normal.

The ILH saw little further action, but was with the main advance right up to the end. During the pursuit north, theirs was a war of reconnaissance, manoeuvre, railway protection, skirmish and advance. On average they marched fourteen to seventeen miles a day for 300 miles through the desert. Sand got into everything and thirst was the greatest enemy. As part of their rearguard action, the Germans poisoned the water wells with dead animals and sheep dip. Despite warning notices being put up, it was considered to be unethical because of the suffering of the horses.

In command of the Northern Force was General Louis Botha. His philosophy, derived from experience in the Boer War, was that a mounted commando needed no lines of communication and he applied the commando practice of moving at the speed of the fastest man. As soon as the first man was in the saddle, he would move off and the rest would catch up, whereas traditional cavalry wait for everyone to saddle up and form squadrons before setting off. The infantry followed on in a dust cloud.

The formal surrender of all German forces in the territory was agreed upon on the morning of 9 July 1915. In South Africa, a public holiday was granted in celebration. When news of the victory reached the Western Front there were cheers along the trenches. On arrival at Cape Town docks, the troops were greeted by a joyous crowd with much flag waving, but to a large number of Boers in the Orange Free State and Transvaal, they were not returning heroes—just despised tools of Britain.

One colourful stalwart was General Coen Brits. On his return from South West Africa, at the Cape Town docks, he unloaded a small German artillery piece which he had acquired as a souvenir. Despite the protests of a customs official, it ended up on his front porch. His loyalty to General Louis Botha knew no bounds. At the outbreak of the war, when General Botha ordered him to mobilize, Brits had responded: 'My men are ready; who do we fight—the English or the Germans?' Although he initially had no quarrel with the Germans, he changed his mind once he heard that they had referred to him as an 'Englander'.

Oom Coen (Uncle Coen) was fond of the bottle and while on trek, supplies were scarce. On hearing that a trooper had found a bottle of rum, he sent out an invitation to the man to join him for a drink. 'You can't drink with a trooper' cautioned one shocked staff officer. 'Well, in that case', said the general, 'I promote him to lieutenant—get him some stars'. Standing six foot six in his socks, he would greet friends with a slash of his sjambok (a quirt) in lieu of a more formal military salute. Brits went on to play an important role in the East African campaign and again during the Rand Revolt of 1922.

Although the harsh conditions had taken a toll on the health of many horses and men, battle casualties were even fewer than in the 1914 Rebellion and much fewer than in the Rand Revolt of 1922. A total of 113 had been killed or died of wounds. Subsequently, many of those who joined the South African Infantry Brigade went on to suffer greatly on the Western Front but many went back to their farms and families, content with the part they had played. Despite the hunger and the thirst, one ILH trooper spoke of how he discovered the meaning of freedom in the desert, devoid of all possessions and responsibilities.

In light of the sacrifices which were made on other fronts over the ensuing years, a storm of controversy blew up around the awarding of medals for the GSWA campaign. No immediate awards had been made and it was left to a committee to go over the records and decide who should be decorated. According to an article which appeared in the *Cape*

Times in August 1918, medals had been 'bestowed with an altogether too lavish hand'. The affair was characterised as an 'opera-bouffe'. Under the headline 'South Africa Laughs', the article continued: 'Showers of honours there have been in the past, but this list [the honours list] is not an instance of a shower, it is a downpour, a cloud burst, a deluge... South Africa, when it ceases to laugh, will assuredly resent having been made the laughing stock of the rest of the Empire, for this is what it amounts to.'

Ultimately, it was the commander-in-chief, General Botha, who was responsible for the honours list, and his staff argued that hard marching and physical endurance entitled a soldier to be honoured no less than those who have borne their part in hard fighting. Yet the much-coveted MC and Croix de Guerre and even 'the unfortunate DSO', which were supposed to be fighting decorations, had been cheapened. The War Office, General Smuts and even the King of England were drawn into the fray. The King called it 'a storm in a tea cup' and expressed his trust in General Botha's judgement.

CHAPTER 4

Founding of the 'Seventh Skins'

Within two weeks of the conclusion of the South West Africa side-show, the ILH was disbanded and Harry was sailing to England to join his brother who was now a major in the 7th Royal Inniskilling Fusiliers. Those who travelled to England from the colonies to offer their services were more likely to be given a commission than if they simply joined the Dominion forces in their own countries. Many South Africans followed this path.

In his pocket, Harry had a commission sent to him by his brother, granted by Lieutenant-General Sir Laurence Parsons Bart who had the Aldershot command. He could have travelled first class with all expenses paid by the British government, however, several friends who had served with him in the ILH were travelling in third class and he decided to travel with them. It was not the same as travelling in peace time as the majority of passengers were mainly men who were going overseas to join up. Restrictions were relaxed between classes allowing one to visit whomever one wished. After being exposed to the elements of the desert and sleeping under the stars on stony ground, the third class accommodation did not seem too bad.

After having berthed in Plymouth, Harry disembarked late in the evening and it was from this point that his narrative diverged from the ordinary:

I with three others whom I had met on board ship put up at the hotel and celebrated our return to England, in my case, after a lapse of eight years, with a champagne supper of cold roast sirloin of beef and cold grouse. The roast beef was the roast beef of old England and the grouse reminded me of the moors of Scotland. With as much Veuve Cliquot as we could drink, it was a fitting return to my native soil.

Our party was an unusual one. The host had lost his left hand and wore a black mitten on the stump of his arm. Another member of the party was an elderly man who was an engineer and had been a manager of De Beers in the early days. The third was an ex-armourer sergeant. A queer trio. The elderly engineer told me in confidence that the man with the black mitten, whilst managing a machine shop of some kind had insured himself against accidents then caused his hand to be severed at the wrist. He received a large sum of money in compensation. The armourer sergeant had some uncut diamonds concealed in a bag strung around his neck. These he had gathered on the coast north of Swakopmund during the campaign in South West Africa. It was his intention to form an expedition to this part of the coast which was largely unexplored.

The next morning, I joined my three friends of the previous night and after breakfast we caught the train for Paddington Station. The passing scenery, a patchwork of hedges and fields, classic stone cottages and sleepy villages stirred forgotten emotions in some of us. On arrival, the man with one hand booked rooms for us at a house opposite the station for bed and breakfast. It was not exactly swagger lodging. There were no baths, and each morning, I walked across the street in my dressing gown to Paddington Station cloakroom which was equipped with first rate bathrooms. I stayed in London for a few days and then got in touch with Alex who was with his regiment at Woking.

I wrote to Alex, telling him I was coming down to Woking to discuss joining his regiment in accordance with his suggestion. It had not occurred to me to make any other choice. The newspapers at this time were full of propaganda for recruiting purposes. It was the express policy of the armed forces to post brothers to the same regiment and it seemed to me to be a happy thing to do. But in hindsight perhaps it was not as desirable as it seemed. Generally speaking, one finds from experience that the infantry has a more limited outlook than other arms of the service. The field artillery for instance might have been a better choice for someone who had served in a mounted regiment.

The upshot of my visit was an interview with General Parsons and I went to Aldershot the next day. General Parsons was one of the senior generals in the British army at that time. He was considered by the army council too old for France and had been given the important home command of Aldershot. After passing through the hands of several ADCs, I at length found myself alone with General Parsons. He was a small man with a kindly and pleasant manner which in no way suggested the importance of his position. He was impressed when I mentioned the ILH, saying 'It is our best colonial regiment'. He was thinking of the Boer War days when the ILH had a very fine reputation amongst Imperial army officers who generally considered colonials to be ruffians.

Now General Parsons asked me, 'What would you like to do. I am forming new regiments and could give you the rank of full Lieutenant in one of them. Your brother's regiment, the 7th Inniskillings has now done twelve months training and is due to leave for France very soon. They are up to strength but I could appoint you to this battalion only as a 2nd Lieutenant.'

Surprised at being given the choice, and being ignorant of these matters, I stuck to my original decision saying 'Thank you general, I wish to join my brother's regiment'. Many times thereafter, I considered that I had made the wrong decision. Had I accepted the general's offer of a higher rank, I would have at once got additional pay and a period of some months in England to receive a thorough course of instruction at an officers' training school which was essential for temporary officers. Also, if I had not been in such a hurry, the thought of a commission in the artillery might have presented itself. However, it is not possible to know in a war which decision is best for yourself in the long run and which is worst. Providence decides.

When the new 'service' Battalions were raised in Ireland, the senior officers were initially all British rather than Irish—due to the lack of experienced officers. The Royal Inniskilling Fusiliers had a strong Catholic influence even though they were officially non-sectarian. The regiment's heartland was Enniskillen, Omagh and other towns in the counties of Fermanagh and Tyrone. Traditionally, a regiment would have a number of battalions which would be split between two or more divisions. When at full strength, a British battalion had around 1,000 officers and men divided into four companies of 227 men as well as the battalion headquarters. In reality, numbers fell far short of this and recruiting was not going well by the end of 1915.

The 7th Royal Inniskilling Fusiliers formed part of the 16th (Irish) Division and included both Ulster and southern-based regiments. In the division, there were three brigades (the 47th, 48th, and 49th). With a stretch of the imagination, the brigade could be described as a family group comprising four sister battalions. Within the 49th Infantry Brigade, the four siblings were the 7th and 8th (Service) Battalions of the Royal Inniskilling Fusiliers plus the 7th and 8th (Service) Battalions of the Royal Irish Fusiliers. As a family, they lived together, moved together and shared the same bleak future.

Using the same analogy, it can be said that the division was the extended family and was as much part of the soldier's identity as his regiment. Uniquely, the 16th (Irish) Division was also known as the 'Irish Brigade'. The term 'Irish Brigade' was inspired by the so-called 'Wild Geese' who were a brigade of Irish mercenaries which served in the French Army between 1690 and 1792. This association was the brain-child of General

W. B. Hickie who took over from General Parsons and also personally designed the Irish Brigade Parchment Certificate, a bravery award unique to the division. Incidentally, a representation of the letters LP was painted onto sign boards at the transport HQ in a tribute to Lawrence Parsons. The trucks of the 16th Division were also adorned with the image of a shamrock. Divisional headquarters was in Dublin. The 49th Infantry Brigade was established in October 1914 in the south of Ireland at Tipperary Barracks. By coincidence, the music hall song 'It's a long, long way to Tipperary' became a universal marching song, immensely popular with everyone—except those who had become totally cynical.

Because Harry joined the unit only after it had moved from Ireland, he missed out on some aspects of training and was not there when the bonds of brotherhood were formed. Alex was one of the most experienced officers in the battalion and it was left to him to instil discipline and give courses to the junior officers on tactics, topography, writing reports, billeting schemes and map reading. The routine during training was squad drill and physical training in the mornings with lectures or a route march in the afternoon. Instruction in trench digging was considered to be constructive, and bayonet drill was another favourite obsession as it helped instil a hatred of the Boche and 'arouse the pugnacity of the men'.

According to an article in the regimental magazine, *The Sprig of Shillelagh*, Alex made it a personal goal to develop an *esprit-de-corps* in the battalion. To this end, he lectured the men on the origins and the history of their regiment, assuring them that they were entitled to share in the glory of the past. No doubt he reminded them of the Battle of Waterloo where a battalion of Inniskillings had famously stood firm while being shot to pieces by French artillery. Consequently, they were described as 'lying dead in a square'. More recently, during the Anglo-Boer War, the Royal Inniskilling Fusiliers had again won glory at high cost during the assault of a steep and strongly-fortified hill outside Ladysmith.

Leisure activities, as always, played a vital role in building team spirit, and gave the men an opportunity to get to know each other in a relaxed environment. There were sports days and cross-country races but the most enjoyable of leisure pursuits was the so-called 'smoking concert' which mainly entailed sitting around listening to musical ensembles, discussing politics and smoking. On these occasions, the jovial young Captain Robert Goodman Kerr was a leading light.

Groups of friends who had joined up together and formed strong bonds during training did not take kindly to being split up. When a draft of 300 men from the 49th Brigade was dispatched to reinforce the 10th (Irish) Division, it led to a small mutiny. Alex and other senior officers were incensed at this poaching of their most highly trained men, but the day would come when the 7th Inniskillings had to cannibalise other battalions.

From Tipperary, the battalion went north by train to Ballyshannon in County Donegal, west of Enniskillen, on the coast. Finner Camp was only a two mile march from the station and the route was lined with people, clapping and waving flags. One who was there recalled how it warmed the blood to be part of a marching battalion, with fife and drums playing.

The bracing sea breezes at Ballyshannon did much to acclimatize the men to cold weather, but after almost a year of exhaustive training, they were itching to get over to France and get to grips with the enemy. When the time came to leave Ireland in September 1915, the townspeople and families were invited to an 'at home' day at the camp. The regimental band and Irish pipers played to the public throughout the day.

Company commanders had by now been appointed. Alex, was given 'C' Company. The three other company commanders were Captain V. H. Parr, Captain R. G. Kerr and Captain C. H. Stainforth. Headquarters staff included the Quartermaster, Lieutenant W. Reid, who was one of the few members of the battalion who survived to the end of the war. The original transport officer was Lieutenant T. F. Hazell, but he later transferred to the Royal Flying Corps and Harry was appointed to this post. Lieutenant (Later Major) Tom Falcon Hazell became one of the top scoring aces of the First World War. With 41 victories, he was ranked after Albert Ball VC, MC, DSO and two bars, who had 44 victories. Albert Ball was just twenty when he was killed but Hazell survived the war and died in 1946.

It was indeed a close-knit family which Harry found in the officers' mess when he came in from the colonies. At first, he had difficulty fitting in with his brother officers, for reasons which are best described by Harry himself:

Alex was a regular army man, he was also adjutant and second in command of the battalion. I naturally had to fraternize with a lot of young subalterns who had already had a long period of training. My service in a colonial mounted regiment in a mobile war was not quite the same thing as infantry training in the British army. The young man in Britain differs from the Britisher who lives in the colonies. In the colonies, there is a spontaneous camaraderie which one gets used to and on returning to England, one is aware of an atmosphere of suspicion almost amounting to animosity. In my case, possibly it was thought that a newcomer of an age beyond schools and universities who had seen something of the world might obtain some advantages to which, in the opinion of junior officers, he was not entitled to, particularly if his brother was of senior rank.

An amusing episode, which is said to have occurred in South West Africa, clearly illustrates how the South African attitudes to rank differed from that which was encountered in the British Army. According to the legend, an inexperienced junior officer had been told by a trooper to 'go to hell'. The lieutenant got his commanding officer on the phone and asked what he should do. The voice on the other end of the line responded 'don't go old boy, don't go'.

A few days after Harry's arrival at Inkerman Barracks, major changes occurred in the division. Two brigades were sent to France but the 49th Brigade was still not up to strength and was sent from Woking to Bordon, a training area about ten miles south of Aldershot. The march to Bordon Camp was made memorable by a cold autumn rain. Here the training was particularly monotonous since much time was devoted to digging model trenches, practicing manning and relieving trenches and lectures on trench life. As a result of the efforts of the battalions which trained there, the Bordon countryside had a formidable system of trenches, support trenches and redoubts to rival the real front lines.

The highlight of this period, although it meant a week of marching practice, was a visit to Aldershot by Her Majesty Queen Mary, accompanied by Prince Albert, where she inspected the troops on 2 December 1915. King George was unable to attend as he had apparently had an accident. Among those on parade was the 1st South African Infantry Brigade which was temporarily attached to the 16th (Irish) Division. After the march-past, the Queen drove around the lines and asked to see 'Nancy' the springbok—the mascot of the 4th South African Infantry Regiment.

Bordon Camp was indeed the height of boredom, but within easy reach of London which was full of Dominion troops. Apparently, the higher a regiment's status in the military hierarchy, the closer to London it would be based. Christmas was spent in camp, and bungalows were decorated with holly and mistletoe. Captain Kerr organized one of his successful smoking concerts for the men. Music was provided mainly by regimental musicians, but some professional artistes were also brought in from the Three Arts Club in London. For many, this would be their last Christmas. On Boxing Day the 7th Battalion played against the 8th Battalion in a highly competitive game of football. On the last day of 1915, the officers invited their friends to a 'guest night'. Around midnight, the subalterns took over the fife and drum band to welcome 1916 with a feeble rendition of Sprig-of-Shillelagh.

In January, the 7th Battalion received a draft of about 200 fully trained men. It was now 900 strong and ready to go. During final preparations, the battalion was given a single anti-gas drill on the parade ground, and two PH Helmets (gas masks) were passed around for the men to try on.

Typically, this exercise ended up with boy soldiers grunting animal noises at each other, but they would soon regret not having taken their anti-gas training more seriously—despite the dubious value of these hideous masks. In what sounded ominously like an extolment to self-sacrifice, Father Bernard Vaughn gave a final lecture with the message being: 'Be the best man in the battalion, of the best brigade of the finest division in the British Army.'

CHAPTER 5

Forging of the 'Fighting Seventh'

Just a day or so before departing for France, the commanding officer, Lieutenant-Colonel Hughes and the second in command, Major Lynch-Blosse, both of Boer War vintage, were told that they were too old for front line service and Lieutenant-Colonel Herbert Nugent Young assumed command of the 7th Battalion. His nickname was Oxo on account of his size and powerful physique. On 16 February 1916, the 49th Brigade left Borden station to join the other two brigades of the 16th (Irish) Division across the Channel.

As they left the dock at Southampton, a band was playing Sprig-of-Shillelagh, the rousing regimental marching tune. Accommodation on board the SS *Mona Queen*, a paddle steamer, was limited. A few of the more senior officers were given a bunk but seasickness recognized no rank. A day was spent lying offshore and when it rained, those on deck got drenched by the icy rain. No food or drink was served to the men. It was only while waiting for the train at Le Havre that they were given a cup of tea and a bun—but their hardships and deprivations had just begun.

As millions of Tommies soon learned, the French troop trains made no distinction between men (other ranks) and horses. Officers were given slightly more comfortable carriages. It is written in the official history of the battalion that during a long halt just outside Calais, the regimental mascot (a dog named Rif) jumped off the train and was never seen again. It appears that Alex was the only one who knew what really happened, and his secret is revealed in verse—the very first which he transcribed from scraps of paper into his diary. It may not have been his best literary endeavour, but it may well be a mirror to his emotions as he left behind the familiar and approached the ever more menacing front line. There are no distinct verses—just a continuous outpouring of grief:

To Rif:
(Written on the death of a favourite dog)
Never again those little feet
Will patter on the sand.
Never again those eyes shall greet
Nor soft tongue lick my hand.
For yesterday upon the track
O'er took your careless way
A locomotive super-huge
And claimed you for its prey.
What thoughts did then your mind engage?
What fate had dulled your sense
Was it not given you to gauge
A danger so immense?
Returning to camp with pleasuring thoughts
To meet your welcoming bound,
And chancing to look upon the track
Two severed paws I found
With honour stooping to the Earth
'what dogs are there?' I cried
And then your little quivering form
Crouched in the grass I spied
No sound of pain!
You knew to play
The steel tried heroes' past
No sound of pain!
I only read
The anguish in your heart
No dimming film o'ercast your eye
Facing there deaths dark mood
A helpless trunk, not dead, to die
You knew, you understood.
I could not bring my gaze to meet
Those eyes so deep, so true
Now turned in questioning pain to greet
The voice of him you knew.
Your quivering paw I gathered up
And bore it to a friend,
Beseeched him mercifully to shoot
And so your misery end.
Farewell old Rif! I cannot stay
To share the final blow-

One glance into those pleading eyes
Sadly I turn and go
T'is o'er though not gone from out my life
Sweet noble, tender brave
Thy agile form is still for aye
Bound in a narrow grave.
If nobleman for human kind
Speaks of a high degree
Then surely noble dog
I find
Fit epithet for thee.

After twenty one and a half hours, the train journey ended at an industrial siding called Berguette Station. From there, it was a ten mile night march along an icy road. A thick covering of snow lay over the countryside. Having had very little food for 35 hours, strong men were falling out and some tried to jump on to passing artillery limbers. Together with Lieutenant G. A. C. Walker, Alex went ahead to organize billeting in the village of Nédonchel. Stragglers were still arriving well after midnight. A relaxing three days were spent in this quiet area enjoying the hospitality of the local residents. Continuing their journey eastwards towards the Loos Salient, the next stop was at L'Ecleme, six miles west of Béthune—close enough to the front to hear the guns speak and see flares bursting.

Evidence of war began to blight the scenery. This was one of the most desolate of the war-stricken regions. It was, and still is, a centre of mining and industry—not one of nature's beauty spots. The brigade concentrated in Noeux-les-Mines, close to the ruined village of Mazingarbe where so many from the 16th Division were to be buried in the Philosophe British Cemetery. It was here that Father William Doyle, the Catholic chaplain of the 8th Royal Inniskilling Fusiliers said his first mass in France while long range shells were falling nearby. In his diary and letters to his father, Willie Doyle left a unique account of the struggles of the 49th Brigade.

At 6.00 p.m. on 2 March 1916, all four battalions of the 49th Brigade, less the transport and headquarter staff, left their quarters at Noeux-les-Mines, and went forward to the firing line. The recently captured town of Loos was held in a salient which meant that the Germans lined the approaches and the town could only be entered at night. As the danger zone was reached, the practice was to form single file and then to advance by twos, twenty paces apart—no smoking. At any moment the straight road could be swept by machine gun fire, forcing everyone to lie flat.

Being unable to distinguish between the sound of imminent death and a distant shell passing overhead, the newcomers flinched or fell flat at every

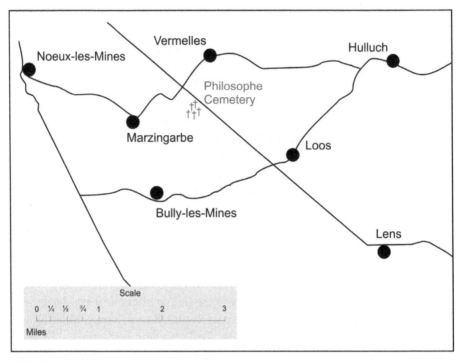

The district of Loos.

juncture. The tired old comments of 'no need to get the wind-up' and 'don't go that way, there's a war up there' were to be expected from the jokers on the side-lines. The Scottish regiments which were being relieved stayed with their charges for two weeks helping them to settle in. Alex's 'C' Company was attached to the 8th KSOB (Kings Own Scottish Borderers) who were seasoned veterans of the Loos fighting. No amount of training could have prepared the new boys for the stench of latrine buckets, rotting corpses, stale human sweat and fumes of cordite. The more pleasant smells of cigarette smoke, frying bacon and wood fires will also be forever associated with the trenches, some of which in this sector were labelled 'Tenth Avenue', 'Broadway', 'The Kink', 'Gordon Alley', 'Quality Street' and the descriptively-named 'Lone Tree Redoubt'.

Tenth Avenue was not an unpleasant place, relatively speaking, although it was infested with rats, fleas, and flies. It was not under direct observation and was seldom shelled. Prior to the first Battle of Loos in September 1915, it had been the German front line and it had been badly damaged. Much work was now being done to improve accommodation and defences. The headquarters dug-out, which was considered to be one of the best and most comfortable 'funk holes', was constructed primarily by the 7th

'Skins' and had been named 'Fort Inniskilling'. In some places, the enemy trenches were only thirty yards away where the unseen Germans could be clearly heard.

In this sector, the land is flat and chalky, the stiffness of the soil permitted the trenches to be dug to a great depth with perpendicular sides. There was not a sign of human life above ground. Men lived like human moles, only coming out at night. There was nothing to see but mud walls, nowhere to sit but on a muddy ledge, no exercise could be taken. Apart from the fear of death or mutilation, the overwhelming impression was one of enclosure, confinement and constraint. The men washed and shaved as best they could but clothes and boots were not removed. Spare time was spent burning the lice from the seams of their tunics—an occupation known as 'chatting'.

The field where the first Battle of Loos had taken place, in September of the previous year, had not been cleared. The ground was littered with unexploded shells, bombs and grenades, broken rifles, torn uniforms and packs. The dead had been hurriedly buried where they fell but severed heads and limbs lay grotesquely about. Father Doyle described how one fellow looked like he had been buried alive for there was every sign of a last struggle and one arm was thrust through the mound of clay. One mound had four pairs of feet sticking out, three Frenchmen and one German—judging by their boots. Such sights were disconcerting and eventually someone would cover the bodies with an old oil sheet or a few scoops of earth. On the wooden cross would be written 'An unknown soldier'. When new headstones were erected in the war cemeteries, the inscription read 'Known to God'—if the nationality was not even known.

Rudyard Kipling's only son, Second Lieutenant John (Jack) Kipling aged eighteen had been killed at Loos on 27 September 1915 after two days at the front serving with the Irish Guards. His body was never positively identified despite a massive effort on the part of his distraught father. Rudyard Kipling had the added anguish which came from having pulled strings to get his son into the army since he had at first been refused entry on account of his poor eyesight.

One of the wonders of the war in this sector was the famous Crucifix, a large cross, standing on a mound in a most exposed position. All around it, the trees and houses had been shattered, a tombstone at its feet was broken in half but neither the cross nor the figure had been touched. As far as Willie Doyle was concerned, it was hard to disregard the presence of God when confronted with such a miracle.

Mazingarbe or Philosophe where the battalion was sent to rest, was only a mile behind the lines—out of the range of bullets but not immune to the odd shell. Walking down the streets of Loos on the other hand, was most unhealthy. Stray bullets and shell splinters wined and clattered on the rubble. Even in the underground shelters, there was the prospect of being buried alive or blown out of the trenches.

The routine for the next few weeks was three days in the trenches and then three days in a village behind the lines. The 7th and 8th battalions rotated with each other. Casualties from enemy action were few, but the frost and snow took its toll through illness. After three weeks of getting used to life in the trenches, the last ten days of March were spent getting to know the French population, well behind the lines. With time on his hands, Alex again turned his attention to his diary:

> This diary is doomed to failure and I have failed to write anything in it since the 9th of April. Let me see—10th Avenue for three nights, on the 12th we moved out to Mazingarbe and have been there since. Moving out again on night of 20/21. The weather has been dirty but shows signs of improvement. No doubt if I stick at the business, I shall eventually be able to write with ease of something—at present it comes hard.

Harry was pleased to find that the life of a transport officer 'was a lucky one'. He did not have to stay in the trenches although he had to go up every night to the front line with transport and rations. As he explained in his memoirs, 'it was not altogether pleasant as one was exposed at times to shell and machine gun fire without being able to take cover, on roads previously marked for attention by the enemy'. Nevertheless, his life was more 'healthy and free'. He had horses to ride and could move about the country during the day when not occupied with supervision and inspections. He certainly did not envy the life of the men in the trenches, especially being able to sleep in relative comfort. While in the trenches, men huddled against the rain with their legs being pushed aside every few minutes by passers-by.

The overriding impressions of the transport lines were of rows of bell tents, limbers, horses switching their tails, loading and unloading limbers, carrying fodder, shouting at horses and mules, strewn with empty shell boxes, used for making fires as well as for building bivouacs. One could see the dirty white tents of the Red Cross camp and troops going to and from their billets.

Some heavy bombardments were directed at the battalion headquarters and observation posts during the first week of April and some valuable lessons were learned about trench warfare. The first awards for courage under fire were given in the form of parchment certificates. These were awarded by the commanding officer of the 16th (Irish) Division to both officers and men. During this period, Alex may have neglected his diary but he did write a short, sarcastic piece for the regimental news magazine— *The Sprig.*

The company commander sat in his dug-out. His last subaltern had just been sent on a course for darning socks. A guttering candle gave the only light that relieved the gloom, and large drops of water fell with a relentless splash here and there and round about it. Indeed, it was a wonder it did not get hit. At one end of the dug-out could be heard the murmurs of servants talking in a low tone over a charcoal brazier, from which was escaping the sizzle and smell of frying bacon; it was near breakfast hour. At the other end, the buzz of the telephone vented its mosquito-like hum in a leisurely way. But suddenly in a flash the buzz-buzz became crisp and decided. A message was coming through buzz—buzz, buzz, buzz.

'What the devil is it now' thought the company commander. In a few minutes a figure loomed up.

'Sir, the Adjutant wants to speak to an officer of the company on the phone.'

'All right, I'm coming.'

From outside. A crash!! Bang!! The dug-out shook with the concussion. 'I ought to go up and see what's going on.'

'The Adjutant is waiting sir.'

Boom! Bang!! Crash!!! The dug-out shook outrageously.

'I must go up, the Adjutant can wait.'

Up above, the parapet was flying about in little pieces. The trench was being shelled by heavies, strafed by rifle grenades, and peppered with pip-squeaks. The company commander sped round and encouraged the men to spread out and take cover. For their part they were more or less indifferent. Here was one frying bacon on a biscuit tin. Bang! Another bit of parapet leaps out and deposits Private McMifty on his back on the floor of the trench.

'Begorrah Sir,' says he, 'they've put me off my seat.'

For twenty minutes, the company commander darts up and down the trench. Then the strafing ceases.

'Thank God no casualties,' he says, as he wipes the sweat off his brow and returns to the dug-out.

The Adjutant is again calling up with obvious irritation.

'The CO wishes to know why there is no officer at the phone.'
'Yes.'

'Tell him we were being strafed.'

'Yes, had to go on deck.'

'Yes, no other officer available.'

'Yes. By the way, what is it you want?'

'CO wishes you to detail an officer for a course of instruction in the use of trench gloves.'

Fizz! A larger drop than usual has registered a direct hit on the candle, and all is darkness and stifled words in the dug-out.

Clearly Alex was being sensitive to the feelings of his uninitiated readers as he declined to portray the torment which had to be endured during a strafing episode. It would have been more edifying had he attempted to describe the effect of heavy shells on vulnerable flesh and blood and the misery inflicted on the spirit. To be sure, there was no 'humbugging' about the bureaucratic demands of Brigade or the tendency of sending subalterns on time-wasting courses.

Even Walker, the regimental historian, who was usually unforthcoming on these matters, conceded that morale was negatively affected by the German trench mortars or *Minnenwerfers* known as 'Minnies'. One could actually see these agents of death as they approached, with no hope of getting out of the way. The detonations were deafening and deadly. The most effective response was to shell a section of the enemy line mercilessly so that they might put pressure on their own mortar sections to desist. A deep dug-out offered reasonable protection against all but the heaviest shells, but the trenches themselves would be wrecked. Against a direct hit there was no salvation and on occasions, Delville Wood for example, every square foot of soil would be churned up.

It was strangely and eerily silent for a few days and then on the evening of 26 April 1916, the Germans opened up their preliminary bombardment which was a prelude to a terrible gas attack. The attack was largely unexpected but had they been observant, the Irishmen would have noticed that the rats deserted the trenches a day or two before the cylinders were opened. In the Hulluch sector, just north of Loos, the first cloud of gas blew over at 4.45 a.m. on 27 April 1916. The 7th Royal Inniskilling Fusiliers bore the brunt of the attack. The gas drifted as far back as Mazingarbe and much of the artillery fire was directed against the batteries there. Throughout the next few hours, the shelling intensified and the German infantry attacked in strength.

The Lewis gun teams kept their composure and inflicted many casualties on the attackers coming across no man's land but one raiding party managed to get into the Irish trenches at the junction of 'B' and 'C' companies. Some were taken by surprise and captured, while others fought off the enemy hand-to-hand. While being escorted across no man's land to the German lines, unlucky prisoners and their captors were killed by shell fire from the British side. By now, 500 British guns were firing and the noise had reached a crescendo. Further waves of gas and infantry attacks were attempted but were not successful. Colonel Young's report stated that at 11.15 a.m., a German aircraft crashed 800 yards behind battalion headquarters and by 11.30 a.m. the sector was silent. The plane lay like a dead locust and there was no movement under the wreckage.

Sickly sweet fumes of poison gas still hung over the trenches, killing even the insects. Everywhere, wounded and gassed men staggered back to aid posts supported by comrades. Many did not have their masks with them or they had been lost or torn as it was thought that the Germans had given up on the gas. In any case, the early sack-type gas masks were ineffective. In an effort to breathe, the dying had ripped their clothes and scratched their faces. The valley was filled with a long low moan from those struggling for life. Such was their agony that some men shot themselves. After dark, patrols were sent into no-man's land to bring in anyone still living. German bodies were searched for identification and souvenirs. Parties of prisoners were escorted to the rear, some of whom did not make it to safety—the Irish boys were enraged and took their revenge.

Out of a total of 24 officers and 603 other ranks who went into the line, 10 officers and 203 other ranks were casualties (66 of whom were killed). In this action, the division as a whole suffered 1,980 casualties of whom 1,260 were victims of gas.

Messages of congratulation and medals were lavished on officers and men and on the battalion as a whole. From now on, the battalion would be known as 'The Fighting Seventh'. A glowing piece appeared in *The Times* which described how the enemy was put to rout by the Royal Inniskillings who came up from the reserve trenches at the double. 'Never was a job more quickly and more cleanly done', added the war correspondent. Alex, along with 20 other officers and men, was presented with the 'Parchment of the Irish Division' in appreciation for 'services rendered and magnificent behaviour' during the gas attack at Hulluch. For some reason, he declined to write anything about this episode.

CHAPTER 6

'Rest', Raids and Religion

After their gas ordeal, the depleted battalion was relieved by the 7th Camerons and moved back to Philosophe to recuperate. Not much rest was had amidst the reorganization and cleaning up. All metal objects including rifles and brass buttons had to be polished as they were covered in grime from the gas. In addition, fatigues parties were detailed to carry rations and equipment to the front system and to carry out repairs to the trenches which had been seriously damaged. These activities took place at night and involved a five mile trudge to and from the trench zone. Not surprisingly, pioneer work sapped morale and one could never feel completely at ease.

Even behind the lines, officers enforced discipline without mercy and in the orderly room, the paper war carried on without abating. Alex's diary entry of 17 April 1916 is in the form of a light-hearted ditty—which he tells us was directed specifically at platoon commanders, poking fun at the censorship regulations:

'CENSORED'

More careful in the trenches trough
Because tonight we're going off
We sing hooray! That we're away
To peaceful ~~Philosophe~~.
Turning our thoughts to other harbours
Where we shall get both bath and barbers
Off we go, on eager toe
To dirty ~~Mazingarbe~~.
Or we shall have the chance to preen
Ourselves, and swank our shoulders green

In town of rest that we like best
Dear noisy ~~Noeux les Mines~~.
These are the three rest havens where
When from the trenches we repair
We lay our heads on feather beds
And rest while we are there.
REST!—a great word for tired men
Take off our boots and clothes and then
'neath blankets dry, to droop an eye
Until this clock strikes ten
If that were true it might be so
Platoon Commanders answer 'NO!'
'Give us the stench of any trench'
'THE REST we will forgo'
'____ ALL FATIGUES let us repair'
'Back to the firing line, for there.'
'Though sleep is shy and danger nigh'
'We're used to wear and tear'.
'We came, the Hun, the Bosche to fell'
'The firing-line-it suits us well'
'This shifting dirt—it does not hurt'
'But is it restful?'
'Such work let chosen diggers do'
'Objectors conscientious too'
'They're spurned the right to come and fight'
'Make them a drudging crew.'
'We do not grouse to do our bit'
'We do not make a boast of it'
'But if we fight, we've earned the right'
'To stop and rest a bit'.
'A blightie or a khushi, so____'
'The only rest that we can know'
' Then even that denied us flat'
'Let bullet lay us low'

Silly little ditty it may be, but it expresses the way fighting men felt
at having to carry out fatigues and other work which should have been
done by the pioneer companies or perhaps by conscientious objectors.
In spite of the sentiments which he expressed, it was most likely to
be Major A. D. Reid himself who insisted that the battalion carry out
parades with peacetime punctiliousness and smartness during periods of
so-called rest.

Inevitably, officers who shared the danger and hardship with their men shared a close bond on the Western Front. Social incompatibilities were smoothed over by shared discomfort. Nevertheless there was still a wide distinction between officers and men. All officers, even subalterns, had a batman—more commonly called a servant. The ruling classes did not become too familiar with their servants. Those who had breathed the liberated air of the colonies were not as class conscious—within their own race group.

Whereas men marched, company commanders and the colonel rode well-groomed horses, looking superior—it was the natural order of things. In the beginning, line officers dressed very differently from the men. Officers wore riding boots or leather puttees and riding breeches and never carried a rifle. However this made officers a target and in the firing line, infantry officers eventually discarded all signs of rank. One indispensable sign of rank was the swagger stick. In Irish regiments, this short riding crop or shillelagh was usually made from blackthorn with an engraved silver top.

Old soldiers who had been at Loos and the Somme commanded respect and their faded, crumpled uniforms were a source of pride. Staff officers on the other hand, were typically despised by fighting men. They wore bright scarlet cap bands and scarlet tabs on their lapels—hence the term 'Red Tabs'. It was suspected that many of the ill-conceived, arrogant orders which were issued by them had little merit other than to render the maps on the walls of their vast châteaux more symmetrical. They spent much of their time dining in fine restaurants in Amiens and Boulogne and showing visiting politicians and dignitaries a sanitized version of the battlefield.

Professional soldiers, particularly cavalry officers with their superior social connections, looked down on temporary or 'opportunist' officers who would not have been welcome in the regiment in peacetime. In peacetime, a candidate for a commission would have to have an independent income which would enable him to play polo and hunt and keep up the reputation of the regiment. Temporary officers had to attend courses where one of the lecture topics was 'conduct befitting officers and gentlemen'. In the early days, subalterns were called 'warts' and were never spoken to by senior officers—except on parade.

During the last week of June, Alex was granted leave to England which he enjoyed in near isolation. Certain officers would have been disappointed at the lack of salacious stories on his return. This was a journey back to the happy places of his childhood. Four nights were spent in Scotland, where he had some fishing in the River Deveron, one night spent travelling and one night in London arriving back in France on 29 June 1916. The supply of whisky which he brought with him, no doubt from the Dufftown-Glenlivet distillery, would have delighted the members of his mess.

Between the major offensives and especially during the build-up to the Somme offensive, raids were carried out on enemy trenches—a most stressful activity. Not much was ever achieved apart from harassment and keeping the Hun occupied. Sometimes the purpose was to capture a prisoner (for intelligence purposes), sometimes to inflict as much damage as possible and leave, or sometimes to gain ground. Unpleasant encounters were likely to occur in no man's land. Both sides wanted to control no man's land, to be able to establish listening posts and redoubts. By all accounts, it was a nerve-racking business, tiny noises were magnified a hundred fold. The most intelligent and courageous men were usually chosen for a specialized raid, and much planning went into it. As far as the fighting men were concerned, raids were unnecessary suicide operations—prisoners would sometimes refuse to talk or they knew nothing or gave false information. The Red Tabs on the other hand were not unduly worried about casualties during otherwise quiet periods. A high casualty count in a particular division or brigade signified aggression and the commanding officer would improve his chances of a DSO.

Colonel Young, who gained the distinction of a DSO and bar, was forever thinking up schemes to annoy the enemy and during rest periods specialist teams were trained in the art of trench raiding. In the vicinity of 'Noeux' on the night of 9 May 1916, a massive dummy raid was carried out and the accompanying bangs and flashes may have led some villagers to think that the Boche was upon them. Alex commanded the 'raiding party' and was ultimately put in command of a special company totalling fifty men which was selected for raiding purposes. Although he conscientiously carried out his task, it can be seen from his notes that he was a sceptic as far as raids were concerned:

These small raids are played out. They are all organized on the same lines and come as no surprise to the enemy who are on every occasion waiting for the raiders somewhere behind their wire.

No useful results are achieved, and the cost is a heavy casualty list—probably far higher than the other side.

The only really successful raids as far as one can judge from the reports and from speaking with officers of battalions that have carried out raids, are those which have received very careful preparations lasting over 8 or 10 days.

The latest reports show that the Germans block their front line, hold the leads of their boyaux [communication trenches] with strong posts and with machine guns concealed in the parados [fortification behind a trench, giving protection from being fired upon from the rear] with exists to the rear. On the alarm of a raid being given, they man the support line in strength and open a heavy fire with rifle grenades or even artillery on their own front line as soon as they think that we have got in there.

The question then is how to organize a successful raid against this method of defence.

First of all it is obvious that to get to grips with the enemy and take prisoners we must make a determined attempt to force our way through his front line defence and penetrate into his support line in sufficient strength to drive him back from a portion of his trench there, while we occupy it for a certain time, retiring in good order after having attained our object.

The following factors are indispensable:

1) Artillery barrage must be adequate.
2) Trench mortar and stokes guns must be assigned definite targets and the greatest care taken to ensure their ranging is accurate.
3) A storm of rifle grenades should be arranged to fall in the support line, to cover the advance. The rifles being carried out into No Man's Land. Angle of fire having been previously obtained by careful measurements taken from an aerial photograph and checked by observation.
4) Parties must be assigned their particular work and each man must thoroughly understand his job.
5) Strong blocking parties must be left at boyaux heads on flanks of portion of line to be raided.
6) The advance need not necessarily be confined to the trenches. But this is a point that is open to discussion.

The following is a sequence of preparations and events:

1) Company commanders are given aerial photographs of the front line. These are carefully studied by scale. The first night officers patrols are sent out to make a careful examination of the ground in no man's land and choose shell holds or suitable sites for grenade rifles. Points where enemy wire is narrow are carefully marked and a full report sent to OC raid.
2) Next day company commanders make a careful survey of German line with number 14 periscope identifying if possible of boyaux, MG emplacements etc.

    Meanwhile the OC Raid is also busy making a personal survey of our front line, no man's land, German front line, comparing the ground with aerial photographs and getting an accurate picture of the locality into his mind.
4) As soon as reconnaissance has been carried out as far as practical, preparations are made on the third day, and on the third night and morning of the fourth day the raid takes place.
5) Preparations include the following:

a) Selection of assembly point.
b) Selection of headquarters OC raid and laying of temporary signal communication.
c) Testing all communications.
d) Discussions.

Unlike some less aggressive formations, the 16th (Irish) Division never missed an opportunity to disturb and annoy the enemy, and the unseen Red Tabs to the rear were making a name for themselves through their raiding activities. On the night of 15/16 June, while the 8th Battalion was relieving the 7th Battalion, a disastrous raid was carried out with the intention of determining the identity of the troops opposite and to bring back prisoners if possible. Less than a day was given to planning. A new weapon, the Bangalore torpedo, was to be used to blow a gap in the enemy wire. A Bangalore team was provided but none of the planners had ever seen a Bangalore and knew nothing of its capabilities or limitations.

While Colonel Young and the adjutant worked through the afternoon planning every detail, Alex picked the two officers and forty men who were to go under the wire. The first party was led by Second Lieutenant H. B. O. Mitchell who was an experienced veteran and had already won the Military Cross. The second party incorporating the Bangalore section was led by Second Lieutenant J. B. Watson—a new arrival. The prospect of a raid was apt to cause a hollow feeling in the stomachs of the staunchest of men and the entire HQ would be diffused with an air of anxiety. It was always the good lads who volunteered or were chosen for these shows.

The section of trench selected was just south of Posen Crater, the site of a previous mine detonation. A body of men from the 8th Battalion went forward to occupy the crater while the raiding party went into the enemy trenches. Before setting out, a group of very scared men gathered around the padre to receive the holy sacrament. Major Rudkin, the Brigade Major had expressed a desire to witness the operation, and he and the CO went up to the firing line to observe. Faces blackened with burned cork, brandishing 'knobkierries', pockets stuffed with Mills Bombs, bantering about 'blighty ones' the raiders vanished into the darkness on all fours.

It was a wash-out. In no man's land, Mitchell spotted a German patrol in the darkness and decided that if the raid went ahead, they would be cut-off on their return, he thus gave the signal to retire, which was a red Verey light. Watson and the Bangalore team started to withdraw immediately but the enemy realizing what was happening, raked their path of retreat with machine gun fire and within five minutes, his artillery was in action concentrating on the trenches to which they were heading. Just yards away from safety, Watson was wounded, and although he was rushed to the aid post, he succumbed to his wounds the next day (the 17th). Feeling personally responsible for what happened, Alex procrastinated for more than a month before writing the obligatory letter of condolence to the Reverend Thomas S. and Anna C. Watson of The Rectory, Carrickmacross, County Monaghan:

28/7/1916

Dear Sir

It was my duty to have written to you a month ago when your son 2nd Lieut WATSON most unfortunately died from wounds received in action on the 16th June. I am sorry that there has been this delay but feel that you will be glad to hear from me who was his company commander during the time when he was in the 7th Inniskillings and who was with him soon after he was wounded.

Your son had many good qualities and had the makings of a good officer. I had picked him out of the subalterns of the company to take charge of a special party that was being trained for a special purpose. He was very cool-headed and had plenty of pluck.

On the night in question he was in charge of a party that had been sent out to blow in the enemy's wire entanglements. He lead his party right up to the German wire, but was forced to bring them back owing to a superior force of the enemy making an attempt to get round him.

He withdrew successfully but as he himself reached our wire being at the rear of his party and seeing that all got in safely he was hit by a hand grenade in the legs and had to be carried in.

When I saw him he made light of it and said 'oh I am alright'.

At the time I did not think the wound was serious. A doctor was on the spot and dressed his wounds and he was carried straight to the field dressing station and thence to the hospital with little delay. He had therefore a better chance than many who have to lie all day in the dressing station before they can get away. Unfortunately it was found necessary to amputate his leg- but already owing to loss of blood and shock doctors say he was sinking.

The other officers of the company his own platoon and myself were present at his funeral, performed according to the rites of his church in the battalion burying ground.

We all regret his loss in the battalion. You will be proud to know that though so young an officer he behaved so gallantly.

A. D. Reid, Major, 7th R Innes Fus

Bluntly put, Benjamin Watson was just a boy of twenty. The life expectancy of a platoon leader, usually a subaltern, was indeed short.

Just how short is illustrated by the fact that during the period of a week at the end of July, no less than twelve new second-lieutenants joined the battalion as replacements. A draft of 100 other ranks, mostly belonging to the Connaught Rangers, also joined while the battalion was behind the lines at Noeux. Another draft of 100 men from Irish regiments arrived the following month.

Life was cheap but the dead were given such honours as military circumstances would allow. Members of the regiment, who were not on working parties or manning the trenches, could attend the funeral. This meant that the transport people such as Harry were often called upon to do the honours. It was rare for senior officers to attend or for the buglers to be on hand to play the last post as was the case at one of the burials that Alex described:

This morning we turned out at 7 a.m. to bury seven of our men (B Coy) who had been killed in the big strafe of Thursday when the front and support line was heavily shelled. My company happened to be in a reserve trench and saw nothing of it, but were sent up at 4 p.m. to do repairs! We did not get back to Philosophe, having been relieved in the afternoon, until 6 a.m.

About the funeral, it was a grand sunny spring morning and the front was peaceful. It was Sunday morning too. Such days are among the few of relaxation in this life. It is true our task was a sad one; but no one can be really sad when the sun is shining and the birds singing and yes, just one violet in blossom. I happened to be standing over it. Some friendly hand had planted it in a newly covered grave, and it had sent out a flower almost at once. The smell of it reached me and took me far away from Philosophe. We shall have quite a noticeable cemetery at Philosophe before we move. There are already 30 buried there. The French government have given over in perpetuity any parcels of ground used as burial places for British soldiers. A man of artistic tastes has put up some simple but well designed wooden crosses painted white with the name in black lettering. The name is also written on a paper, the paper put in a bottle, corked and placed in the earth neck downwards until the bottom is flushed with the soil.

The RC [Roman Catholic] chaplain stood at one side and the C of E (Church of England) at the other—we are a RC battalion but have about 25 per cent other religions. Six of the dead were RC's but the C of E claimed the seniority and read his service first. The officers stood in a row bareheaded between the representatives of the several churches. The men drawn up facing them outside the fence. The services were over in a few minutes, the bodies sewn up in brown government blankets were lowered into the graves. Town buglers played the last post and all filed slowly away. Tonight we move to 10th Avenue to form brigade support for three nights.

It was not always feasible to bury the dead with such dignity. Father Doyle described just how he buried the decomposing corpses from battles past in the Loos area. They were buried where they fell which was within view of the Germans and burials had to take place at night. The grave was dug in the dark and Father Doyle read the service by torchlight, shielded by a group of men with their caps. Two bodies fell to bits when lifted off the stretcher and the burial party had to shovel the remains of the one fellow into the grave.

There is a barrack room ballad which Alex penned in his brown book at this time. There is no knowing how the tune went or whether he composed it himself. It may have been sung to the tune of some well-known song. It has an Irish flavour as in Irish slang a 'buffer' is a mildly derogatory term for a person from a rural area. Undeniably it fits the circumstances of this time and place:

(I)
A 7th Inniskilling lay dying
And as on his death bed he lay
To his comrades, who round him were sighing
These few parting words he did say.
Chorus
Wrap me up in my government blankets
And say a poor buffer lies low, lies low
And four stretcher bearers shall carry me
With steps that are mournful and slow.
(II)
I know I'm not good enough for 'Blighty'
And I don't want to go down below
I wish that the base was not a bad place
For an Inniskilling to go
Chorus
(III)
Then get the six rum jars and soda
And lay them out in a row, a row
Pioneers, police, cooks and the transport
Will drink to the buffer below.
Chorus

(IV)
Put a little white cross for a tombstone
And on it write this tale of woe
If he hadn't forgotten his gas mask
He wouldn't be lying below.
Chorus

The 16th Division included Irishmen of all religions and political persuasions. The rifts and rivalries were put aside when danger threatened, but out of the line, there was a good deal of slagging. It was often said that Irishmen were happy-go-lucky but also temperamental and not to be trusted. It may be true that the Irish soldier was disposed to be foolhardy, heedless of consequences, or more likely, contemptuous of them. Recklessness was in their character. For example, they were apt to take a short-cut along a road swept by shellfire, rather than take the secure but circuitous route along a communication trench. Nevertheless, the Irish regiments, like the Highland Scots regiments, were considered to be 'dependable' and were called upon for important tasks. According to an article in *The Times*, the Irish were the finest 'missile troops' in the British Army.

Indeed, the Irish upheld their reputation on 1 July 1916—the first day of the Battle of the Somme. The 36th (Ulster) Division achieved its objectives when few others did, but no other regiment suffered higher casualties on a single day than the Royal Inniskilling Fusiliers. Of the 4,000 Inniskillings in five battalions, some 2,208 were killed or wounded. The 1st Battalion suffered a casualty rate of 70 per cent in the first half hour. Their forefathers at Waterloo, by comparison, had incurred 61 per cent casualties—almost all from artillery over the course of an afternoon. When the casualty lists appeared in the Belfast papers, there was much wailing in the streets. Meanwhile, in the Loos sector, the men of the 7th and 8th battalions wondered whether they would be for it next.

The regimental newsletter, *The Sprig of Shillelagh,* appeared monthly and contained mainly news of promotions, transfers, deaths and decorations. It was registered at the GPO as a newspaper and was published monthly in Londonderry. In some issues, there were historical articles about wars and battles past. Considerable space was given over to humorous pieces and feeble Irish jokes. Here are a few examples which come in varying degrees of un-funniness:

An English Colonel, at a kit inspection said to Private Flanagan:
    'Ha! Yes, shirts, socks, flannels, all very good. Now, can you assure me that all your articles of kit have buttons on them?'
    'No Sir,' said Private Flanagan hesitating.

'How's that private?'
'Aint't no buttons on the towels Sir.'

Attempts were made to poke fun at and imitate Cockneys, Australians, Scotsmen and even South Africans, but of course, Irish jokes were the perennial favourites:

Sergeant:
  'What is strategy in war? Give me an instance of it.'
Irish Private:
'Strategy is when yez don't let the inimy dischover that ye are out of amunishun, but kape on firin.'

One contributor sent in a piece of advice on how the folks at home could replicate the trench experience:

Choose a very muddy piece of ground and dig a hole four feet deep and two feet wide. Fill it half full of dirty water. Put an old saucepan on your head and a bag of stones on your back, and get into your hole and sit down. It will be more realistic if the gardener comes along with a water-can every half hour and waters you. When it gets dark, the gardener should bring you some corned beef and some biscuits. Let him drop them twice before he deposits them in the mud. About midnight, make him bring two rats and let them loose in your trench. The longer you stay in your trench, the more thrilling it will be.

English and Scottish officers of Irish battalions were sometimes puzzled by the nature of their men with their impulsiveness, wild imagery and expressions. The changing moods of their men, childlike and petulant, now jovial, now fierce and occasionally unaccountable caused exasperation for officers who were invariably formal and precise in matters of discipline. Yet their capacity for fighting, in war time, covered a multitude of imperfections. One English general gave the opinion that the Irish are magnificent fighters but rotten soldiers. When they receive an order to retire, their response is 'damned if we will'. It was said in jest that the only deserters in an Irish battalion were men who left their rear echelon posts to participate in a battle.

The Irish had a reputation of having a delight in fighting which gave them a natural disposition for warfare. A war correspondent related that he met a wounded Irish soldier hobbling back painfully to the field dressing station after a battle, and giving the man his arm to help him on, he was prompted to make the pitying remark: 'It's a dreadful war.' ''Tis indeed Sor, a dreadful war enough,' said the soldier, and then came the classic comment: 'but, sure, 'tis far better than no war at all.'

Father William Doyle noted that the French girls loved the Irish boys for their simplicity, generosity and unaffected piety. Amid the death and destruction, some questioned or even abandoned their faith whereas the Irish Catholics remained resolute. In the words of Willie Doyle, 'It is an admitted fact, that the Irish Catholic soldier is the bravest and best man in a fight, but few know that he draws that courage from the strong faith with which he is filled and the help which comes from the exercise of his religion'.

The Catholics were more likely to believe that prayer turns bullets and that a priest offered better protection than reinforced concrete. Those of other persuasions had the fatalistic attitude that if your number is on it, nothing will save you. Luck played a big part and it was not a good thing to use up one's luck. Almost everyone had stories of miracle escapes and also of premonitions which materialized. Even non-Catholics carried a rosary for luck—and would also be buried with it. To some, a rosary was more than a charm, it was like having someone strong and brave by you. One NCO who found himself all alone in a trench, with only a barrier of sandbags between himself and the Germans related: 'I had nayther men, machine gun or grenade, nothing, save the help of the Mother of God.'

At every opportunity, staunch Catholics would cleanse their souls by confession—or in the parlance of the Irish soldier, 'scraping one's kettle'. A priority of the Catholic padres was administering last rites to the dying. Under the most trying circumstances, the padre would give a blessing and anoint a sometimes mutilated head with holy oils uttering the words: 'I absolve thee from thy sins, depart Christian soul and may the Lord Jesus receive thee with a smiling benign countenance. Amen.' It seemed to bring relief, and very often death would follow immediately thereafter. Father Doyle thought of the families of 'his boys' and was moved to add 'may God rest his soul and comfort those who are left to mourn him. Thank God that heaven will one day reunite them.'

Before battle, the Catholic chaplain would give the whole regiment general absolution, as well as mass and communion for those who came forward. He would ask the men to recite the rosary with him. A host of voices repeated the prayers and recited the words, 'pray for us now at the hour of our death. Amen'. Chaplains shared the dangers and discomforts and many were killed.

Willie Doyle virtually attained sainthood, and the evocative letters which he wrote to his father made him a household name in Ireland. For his bravery at the Somme in September 1916, he was awarded the Military Cross. He was recommended for the DSO at Wytschaete and the Victoria Cross at Frezenberg Ridge, but the latter two were never forthcoming. It is said that his being Irish, Catholic and a Jesuit amounted to a triple disqualification. Never far from the hottest action, Doyle finally met his maker on 16 August 1917. His body was last seen near the crossroads on Frezenberg Ridge, east of Ypres, where it was covered with some stones and debris to mark the spot.

The good sisters at St Anthony's Institute at Locre wrote a letter to Brigade expressing the desire to have Father Doyle's body buried at the convent, but the upshot was that the body was never recovered. Another prominent Irishman from the 16th (Irish) Division was (and still is) buried in the garden at the convent. The 56-year-old Major William Redmond who had served as an MP at Westminster for 34 years, was fatally wounded at on 7 June 1917 at the Battle of Messines Ridge. The story of how Private John Meeke MM was hit twice while carrying Redmond to safety was published in the Belfast newspapers and much talked about at the time.

Perhaps, the consolations of the Anglican Church were not as much in demand at an advance dressing station. According to one medical officer, the padre's work was among the living, not among the dying: 'Very soon he learned that the wounded men want the doctor, and chiefly as the instrument that brings them morphia and ease from pain. And when the wound is mortal, God's mercy descends upon the man and washes out his pain. How should he need the padre, when God Himself is near?'

Many Anglican priests, like Father Hill of the South African Brigade, also did heroic work. Hill was wounded at Butte de Walencourt in October 1916. By the time he reached the hospital in Rouen, his whole right arm was gangrenous and had to be amputated. Within a month, the padre had learned to write with his left hand and could do everything but tie his shoelaces. He wrote to the Army Pensions Board requesting that they stop paying him a pension as he could now manage with one arm. For bringing in scores of wounded men from no man's land he was awarded the MC. Hill used to walk fearlessly erect wearing his surplice with a red cross over his uniform.

It seemed that there was no end to the chaplain's work. Besides burying of the dead, they wrote letters of consolation and helped the illiterate to write to their families. Always a friend to the lonely, at executions they offered prayers and companionship in the condemned man's last hours. At Marzingarbe there was an abattoir building where the unfortunate men were kept before being taken out and shot at dawn. The British Army shot to death around eight so-called cowards and deserters in this place.

At the end of the summer, the 16th (Irish) Division departed the dreadful district of Loos. They hoped to be moved to a more peaceful sector, but this was not to be. Lieutenant G. A. C. Walker was speaking for everyone when he expressed the hope that future residents of Philosophe would hold the little cemetery in esteem and that it would be a reminder of what the Irish, both living and dead, had done there.

CHAPTER 7

Happy Valley—Death Valley

Six months had passed since the battalion had landed in France with no respite from the stress and filth of the trenches—apart from the drudgery of fatigues behind the lines at Mazingarbe. From time to time Mazingarbe was shelled, and on one occasion, on 15 August, while playing sport on a field outside the town, an accurate barrage came down killing and injuring a few. In the third week of August, a route march into the peaceful and picturesque countryside near La Buissière with an overnight bivouac was considered to be a most pleasant change.

On the night of 20 August, the battalion moved into the line for the last time in the Loos sector. On the 24th, the divisional artillery fired off all their remaining ammunition as a farewell from the Irish. The Germans held up a notice saying 'Goodbye 16th Division, we'll give the English hell when they come'—or words to that effect. The next day, the 8th East Lancashire Regiment took over this part of the line.

It was with a spring in their step that the Irish Brigade left Loos on 26 August, the men had no greater burden than their packs. Officially, the destination was a secret but most were under the impression that having done their bit, they were in for a spell of well-deserved rest. Even the senior officers were kept in the dark, only the locals seemed to be aware that the road was leading south to Amiens and the battlefield of the Somme. *En route*, at Lapugnoy, a most refreshing three days of real rest was enjoyed in clean houses surrounded by woods and gentle streams. The men were given baths and clean changes of clothing, and officers insisted on reinstating the regime of spit-and-polish the very next day. Alex's own account of the journey follows in stages:

We marched out of Lapugnoy yesterday at 5.40 p.m., the transport having gone on previously under the escort of 'B' Coy to be loaded up.

There was a slight drizzle but the morning smelt fresh and good and we all felt sorry to be leaving this peaceful rural village.

It fell to me as second in command to scour the village for signs of any men left behind. About the middle of the place, I came on two loiterers, quite lost as far as the battalion was concerned. Being old soldiers, they were full of explanations which had to be cut short and headed along the road.

On arrival at the station, I found more trouble. The headquarters company had no tea. Everything always goes wrong with HQ Coy on account of Sergeant ___. He is only a youngster and has not got it in him to fill the post and also to cater for the HQ mess. He has developed into a kind of errand boy, with powers not usually accorded to that paternity, and unfortunately a poor one at that. I have got rid of him at last and a good man in his place, and so I may hope a lot of the worries of feeding the HQ Company may now be removed. Some of the carriages (covered trucks) for the men are very dirty, having been used for horses and never cleaned out. Owing to the lack of men in France now, the railway stations at any rate those in the war area, are in a sad state of neglect. Captain___ __ who has recently taken over the command of ____Company evidently takes me for a kind of glorified QM or 'deus ex machina'. [In some ancient Greek drama, an apparently insoluble crisis was solved by the intervention of a god, often brought on stage by an elaborate piece of equipment, hence 'god from the machine'.]

At any rate, he comes up with extraordinary demands such as on this occasion—sawdust. I suppose I should take it as a compliment but it is sad to be continually disappointing anyone who has a childlike trust in one's powers. Disillusionment may reduce one's stature more than is fair.

Ominously but unquestionably, the direction of flow turned southwards. Now that their destination was fairly certain, the CO took the opportunity to lecture the officers on the semi-open type of warfare which would be experienced in a major offensive. A lecture on the 'beauty of the bayonet' was in discord with the peaceful farmland. Officers were left anxiously amused after one talk where it was mooted that every one of them would be getting either a silver cross or a wooden one—depending on one's individual luck.

On the march to the Somme, it was a company commander's turn to be on the receiving end of the quick Irish wit. One soldier was falling behind, and by way of encouragement, the officer called out 'Keep up, keep, up. We'll make a Field Marshal out of you yet'. The man answered, 'You're welcome to your joke Sor, but I know well that you'll make a casualty of me soon enough'.

Stations and halts were alive with soldiers of all nationalities, Australians, South Africans, New Zealanders and Canadians. There were Chinese, Indians and Malays manhandling the tons of war material which was stacked beside the line. After a busy night of packing and loading, the battalion entrained at the station of Fouquerolles on 29 August. Loading of wagons and boxing of livestock was chaotic, especially since some of the wagons were too big for the trucks. Being the transport officer, Harry was responsible for the logistics and was at the receiving end of much of the criticism. Alex however seemed to enjoy the day:

> The journey proceeded without accident slowly and quietly. Men sat on the floors of the trucks swinging their legs over the edge at the doors and gazing contentedly at the French scenery, which rapidly became more interesting, more undulating and woody—large rich-looking meadows—and reminded them no doubt, in places, of the 'Green Isle'. Officers passed freely from one compartment to the other outside, and as the parties in the various coaches were continually gathering and separating, and the flow of conversation and laughter went on without cease.

On the top of the train was an observation post where gunners sat with their feet dangling over the edge. Ostensibly, their job was give protection against enemy aircraft. Rattling on towards Amiens, they passed a column, many miles long, of an entire New Zealand Division marching towards the Somme. It was an unprecedented sight. Gangs of German prisoners of war laboured in the fields. Passing through Amiens, the train came to a halt at a small siding called Longeau on the outskirts of the town:

> We arrived at about 5.30 p.m., about one hour and twenty minutes late. Longeau was the name of the station. Here there was more delay. There had been a heavy thundershower just before we left the train—that is, really heavy. It came down in lumps. The result was that on the side of the station from which we wished to escape to the road, we were cut off by a muddy pond about two feet deep. We had a fifteen mile march in front of us, it was not advisable to let the men's feet get wet. Besides, why should we? There was a crude wooden rail on the left hand side with gaps in it and a narrow footpath up the line to the next level crossing on the right hand side. The RTO evidently knew his way about. Was it that it was possible to go through the fence? No, it was not possible, one would then find oneself in a yard which was under the control of the génies [French engineers]: M. le commandant appeared, much saluting, shrugging and bowing. M. le commandant suggested the up the line method. The chef de gare appeared. Was it that it was possible to use

the side of the line for such a purpose. No it was not possible. Too bad. These gentlemen are much embarrassed, you know! However, what can you do? The génies here, they do very little. Why should they not build a bridge. It is their job *enfin*. Bowings, saluting, hand shakings took place once more and all parted amicably. Meanwhile, a British Tommy had waded out with a brush and cleaned the drain. The water ran away and we all got home that night like the woman in the nursery rhyme.

As usual the rank and file had no indication of how far it was to their destination and no food was forthcoming. At first it was hoped that the destination was the town of Corbie, five miles away with its fine church and ample facilities, but they marched straight through Corbie's cobbled streets. Corbie is on the River Somme and is one of the few towns in France whose name is pronounced the same way as it is spelled. 'No matter how one pronounces the name of a town', Harry grumbled, 'there will be some bright fellow with superior knowledge who will correct you'.

Only at 11.30 p.m. in the pitch darkness did the column arrive in Vaux-sur-Somme, a dirty little peasant farming village. It had rained again *en route* and one officer had a raging fever. It was a hard slog, but Alex was one of the officers fortunate to be on horseback and consequently had a different perspective:

It was a grand panorama of rolling country with woods and fields yellow with harvest. Long straight roads with their border of poplars cut through it. On our right hand ran the Somme in a deep and wooded valley. Half an hour out we stopped for tea. It was now 6.30 p.m. and the horses were watered. We spent a peaceful half hour and then on again, a relentless trudge for twelve more miles. The men marched well until near the end. But then the worst cases began to straggle and fall out after a very heavy shower of rain. They had had a long and trying day. At last the final halt came and the men were gradually put into their billets by the advanced party who knew the ins and outs. To us who had wondered into a strange land in the dark and knew nothing except that walls surrounded us, the battalion seemed to melt away. There was a last rattle of the wagons as they turned the corner to the place allotted for their park and the village became silent as the night itself. One wondered if one had really been with a great crowd marching, or whether the echo of their feet upon the road was but the dim memory of a dream.

Billets were invariably primitive and unlit. If at all possible, civilians were not put out of their houses and troops were housed in community halls, deserted houses and barns. An average-sized barn at a French farm would house about thirty men. It appeared that French cows were not at all particular about their accommodation for the typical barn was a rickety and draughty construction. If the straw was deep and the roof sound it made better quarters than anything but a good bedroom. Its chief drawback in the men's eyes was that smoking had to be forbidden because of the straw. In this part of France, farmyards are set out in a horseshoe shape and in the evenings, the men usually crossed the courtyard to the kitchen where they would have a smoke and make friends with the farmer, and buy coffee at a penny a bowl from his wife. While at Vaux, on 31 August 1916, Alex felt the need to complain for a change:

This is not a comfortable billet, and the weather is very wet. However, everyone was grumbling to get away from Loos, and now that we have got what we wanted—it would be too early to start grumbling again. A French agricultural village is not likely to afford much accommodation but the surroundings are delightful, though not to be enjoyed in this rain. Each farm has its yard which contains the dung heap and drains into the street. The flies are bad. The general has gone up to visit the front line so that there is absolutely nothing to do but wait for orders. Inspections of feet and gas helmets are being carried out by the companies, otherwise they are having a complete rest. M___ is acting brigadier and turned up here today and gave us some information but very little. We shall probably move from here tomorrow, but even that is uncertain.

Having taken over the HQ mess, I am oppressed with the care of it. The staff was inefficient. Two have already gone, so we are living from hand to mouth, and I have to think from meal to meal which is trying. In a little while, with a new steady cook, a system will evolve which will only need an occasional touch from me to keep it going.

Further on from the sizeable village of Bray-sur-Somme, hidden in a fold of the undulating land, was Happy Valley. It was a restful place, a far cry from Death Valley about three miles distant. There was more than one Death Valley, but it is believed that the Death Valley referred to here is on the approach to Guillemont. Happy Valley itself was sometimes referred to as Death Valley. It was in this place that the South Africans had concentrated before Delville Wood, and to which they had repaired after being literally decimated.

By now everyone had heard about the epic stand which the South Africans had made in Delville Wood a month previously, and their legend had already started to take hold. Harry could be grateful that he had not joined the 1st South African Brigade as did many of his friends from the ILH. Two brothers who had served with him in the ILH, Arthur and

Frederick Mallett from Queenstown were both killed at Delville Wood but these are just two out of the 763 South Africans who were killed in action, died of wounds or missing believed killed at Delville Wood and Longuval.

Arriving in this sector, where the name of every village was already famous, even seasoned troops were awestruck by all the paraphernalia of war. Dotted about there were observation balloon sections, divisional headquarters, tents, horse lines and ammunition dumps. This was the supply area for the front, mostly immune from shelling but one could see and hear the bursts of heavy artillery and on occasion the observation balloons would be attacked by enemy aircraft. Usually, but not always, the observer would parachute to the ground before the balloon was engulfed in flames.

On arriving at Gibraltar camp, it was found to be swarming with flies but conveniently close to the River Somme to wash off the dust of the march. On their return from the front line, the survivors of many a battle had washed off the grime in the same river. Alex now began making regular entries in his journal and it is apparent that he was still enjoying himself immensely:

Every day that has passed since I last wrote in this book, I have looked for an opportunity to give an account of the days doing. I have failed not to find it, but alas to take it. The 31st was spent in Vaux. It was a pouring wet day. Everyone felt at a loose end as the billets were very uncomfortable and full of flies, there was no temptation to sit indoors. One wandered about restlessly waiting for orders which never came. We knew that our destination was ahead of us. Orders did not arrive until 2.00 a.m. after we had all retired to bed. I was waked by an orderly and wondered as usual when disturbed at midnight whether the battalion had to march at once, as the Germans had broken through. The move was an early one. March off at 7.00 a.m.—fortune favoured us as once more, it was a beautiful day. Nothing could have been more enjoyable than the early morning ride. The road was straight, rising and falling over the capacious bellies of the ground. I had to ride ahead to parcel out the camp. My advance party got into an empty ambulance wagon on its return journey and saved them considerable walking. The road was a busy scene—encampments, French troops training, and small parties of soldiers continually passing on their way back. Motorcycles, lorries, horsemen and parties of German prisoners mending the road, made up a busy scene. All around, the country looked peaceful in the morning sun and only the unusual movement of life told of war. The prisoners for the most part looked well-nourished but sulky or indifferent which was perhaps not un-natural. The camping ground was in Happy Valley about

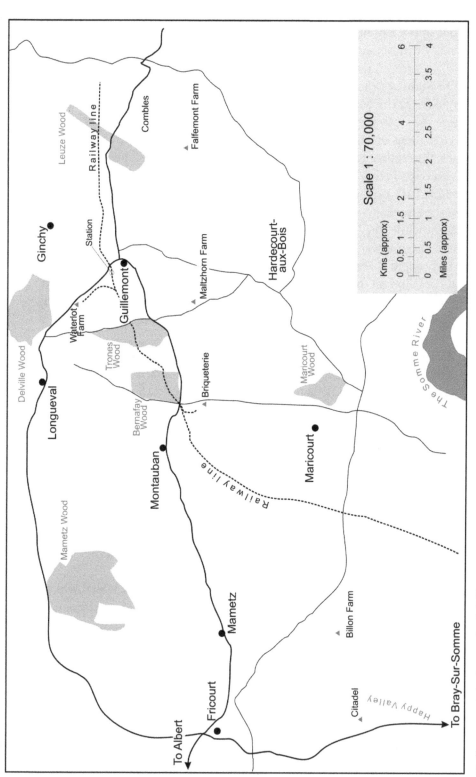

Guillemont and the Somme battlefields.

one and a half miles north of Bray sur Somme. It was a deep, narrow, valley with smooth, bare sides literally swarming with troops.

On Sunday 3 September, the attacking troops, the Connaughts, the Royal Irish, the Munsters and the Leinsters gathered on a bare hillside where the Catholic chaplain administered to them the general absolution given in times of emergency. Then, with green ribbons streaming from their pipes, the regimental pipers gave out inspiring Irish tunes, most notably 'A nation once again' and 'The white cockade', the Jacobite marching tune of the First Irish Brigade in the service of France. It was noon when they went into the attack.

Meanwhile, the 'Fighting Seventh' was moving ever closer to the front where the guns were now a little talkative. Their next move on 3 September 1916 brought them to a camp known as 'The Citadel'—so called because of its position on the top of a hill. Here, there would be some amusements of an evening, but the merriment was an expression of men trying to cling to life knowing that death was waiting around the corner:

We spent part of the 2nd, the 3rd and part of the 4th in this place [Happy Valley], peaceful sunny days, and moved at 4.40 a.m. on the morning of the 3rd about a mile and a half to the Citadel. In Happy Valley we had 40 tents and various shelters which we occupied. The camp was in a filthy state and infested with flies. After we had cleaned up and made everything tidy, the men cheered up wonderfully. We had two impromptu concerts after dinner, a form of entertainment which proved very popular with the men and did a lot to get them in a good fettle. The observation balloons impressed everybody tremendously. We counted no less than 32 up and visible on our front. This was most encouraging after the solitary specimen we were used to at Noeux-les-Mines. Swarms of our aeroplanes came and went bearing information from the front line and hardly ever a German one was seen.

From here I made a trip to the old British and German front lines with two company commanders. Often I had gazed through the telescopic periscope at the outside of the German front line at Loos and wondered what lay behind. Imagination can do a lot but it cannot fill in with a vivid variety of detail and gives a picture of unknown places mostly blurred and obscure. Here at last was the real thing. We descended a deep dugout and examined an underground bomb store. Littering the floor were German overcoats of which all the buttons had been removed already by curio hunters. Mine craters of formidable depth were situated in this part of the line showing the well-made saps by which the Germans had occupied this part of the line.

The Citadel where we moved on the 3rd was similarly situated in Happy Valley, one and a half miles nearer the point. We went into tents and huts and proceeded once more to make ourselves comfortable but our efforts were wasted. At 7.30 p.m. we received orders to move at 8.20 p.m. and had to pack at once leaving a guard on our baggage.

Suddenly, there was no time even to finish a meal. The Battle of Guillemont was underway. All day the battalion had been under orders to move at short notice, and in the evening, the order came to march. All packs including blankets had had to be parked by the side of the road and only fighting kit, consisting of a haversack with three days' rations, two water-bottles, gas helmet, a waterproof trench coat, and usually a book. It was an evocative sight—those packs lined up like that. Not everyone would be coming back to reclaim their kit. The official history records that Major A. D. Reid led the battalion up, and here is his own version of the advance towards Death Valley:

We trekked about 1500 yards across country in the dark by compass-bearing, passed enumerable excitements eventually steering our way by a railway line. Two belching six-inch guns on our left raised six inches every time they fired over our heads. Roaring Lisa was the name of one. It does not seem complimentary to women that guns should be treated as feminine by the Tommy. It is probably less disrespect than a jocular term of endearment. At length we stumbled across some tents, identified the new brigade headquarters. There was no one there. We met some 6th Royal Irish Rifles officers and put ourselves in their hands. The men were pushed into this battalion's quarters in the dark and settled down for the night. Dinner did not arrive until 12.00 p.m.

While the CO and company commanders went forward to reconnoitre, the men were left for a chilly night without blankets at Billon Farm—a farm which existed on the map only as it had been the scene of much fighting at the start of the Somme offensive. As was standard practice, a 'B' echelon was left out of battle. These remained at Billon Farm which became the rear headquarters for the duration of the battle. Alex was one of those to be spared from the initial assault:

We spent the morning [4 September 1916] in identifying our position and visiting cages containing German prisoners, drafts of whom were continually being brought in. But all the time we were alert for our orders to go up to the front line. The RIF [probably Royal Irish Fusiliers] we understood were at the village of Maricourt and had already gone up in front of Falfemont Farm. Later we heard of them being engaged in the attack on that strong point—the preliminary attack on that farm having failed—of their heavy losses, and Major U___ being again wounded and gone home.

About mid-day, the general returned from his tour of inspection. The CO, Adjutant, and company commanders departed to the new brigade headquarters at 'La Briqueterie' (Brickfield) to study the front. I was told to bring the battalion up in the afternoon. The distance was about three miles. Now all was preparation. Our destination was the front line. The men had to carry up all they would require and rations for the next day. We did not know how long we would be up there. Two days, perhaps more—how many of us would return? This was the real thing at last, what we had all been looking forward to.

Between Maricourt, one of the more in-tact villages in this sector, and La Briqueterie there was a battery area where guns of all sizes were creating a cacophony known as 'drum fire'. It was also the dividing line between the British and French sectors and French troops came out of their cellars to watch the Irish pass through the town. Ammunition wagons, ambulances and other transport cluttered the road. The land sloped upwards from Trônes Wood and Bernafay Wood to Longueval village. Before the South Africans had travelled this road on their way to attack Delville Wood, charming houses, enclosed orchards and gardens had once existed in Longueval, with the still verdant Delville Wood beyond. Now it was a mere protuberance on the horizon. On horseback, Alex led the battalion to the assembly point:

At 4.00 p.m. all was ready for the start. We marched off gaily with the band, to run through the repertoire of Irish airs—'Wearin' o' the Green', 'Sprig of Shillelagh' etc. The roads were bad for a mile, more tracks across the open plain, cut up by much traffic, until we reached the main road running straight as a die, lined with tall poplar trees common in France, and paved with rough square stones—pavés. All went well until we drew near the outskirts of Maricourt. Here, although it was only 4.30 p.m., the evening stream of transport had begun to flow and it was only by leaving the main road and taking a cut to the left that we avoided a block and struck the straight stretch of rutted road leading up to the south border of [Trônes] Wood where the trenches and dug-outs sheltering the brigade HQ were situated. Even here it was with some difficulty that the two or three hundred yard column of fours insinuated its length in the thickening traffic. Darkness was already beginning to fall. The band was sent back and we settled down to the serious business of finding an unfamiliar destination in an unknown country. Known to us at least only on the map, which excellent though it may be, cannot mark for insect-like men plodding on foot all the obstacles he is likely to meet—shell pits, trenches, broken wagons, and all the crowding detail and irregularity shown as a quarter square inch of smooth paper.

On we plodded. A steady drizzle had begun to fall which thickened to a silent drenching rain. To add to the discomfort, it was cold. Riding under such circumstances, the discomfort becomes acute. The men carried their overcoats rolled tight upon their belt behind. There was no time to loose and wear them. It was better so. At any rate, they were warm walking. They had still four to six hours trudge before reaching the barren comfort of their destination, a half-dug trench, or none, on a shell-torn hill-side. The coats packed as they were, would be the only dry article they possessed when the sun came out again to dry them. Besides, if they wore them, the heat and exertion would be unbearable and the skirts dipping in the liquid mud would cake and add enormously to the weight they carried.

Yes, far better it was to walk than sit a horse. The rain trickled down my neck. My hands were numb and feet without feeling. The horse too, prickly with discomfort, started at and danced from the shadows. The road was full of deep holes—a false step and disaster. Nor was physical discomfort the only thing to be endured.

Here at last we came in touch with our own artillery, massed in overpowering strength. Away to the rear, two days before, we had stood beside the 6 inch guns belching their shells with monotonous regularity and without pause. We had passed another girdle of guns on our march of this afternoon, but here was a plain stretching on both flanks of the road interminably in the darkness, in depth about two miles sown with British howitzers, their black and gaping muzzles tilted at an ugly angle. Every quarter minute marked with a roar and blinding flash. Close to the road on which we marched to the right and to the left, these flashes stupefied the darkness. A deafening roar or ear-shattering bark from one's very elbow seemed to rend the fibres of my mare.

'Is there a show on?' I asked a gunner.

'No, everything is pretty quiet now,' he answered.

'Quiet? Good God! What is it like when you are busy?'

'A continuous roar' he said.

At last I had reached what I imagined was a stone's throw of our meeting place with the CO and company commanders. It was impossible to remain on the road, now crowded with gunners, service corps and medical, transport, field kitchens, ambulance apparently a seething eddy of confusion. I halted the column and reconnoitred a field to my right. It was now pitch dark. More by feeling than by sight, it was measured to allow room to deploy the battalion. True, it was gashed with shell holes—pits eight foot deep and twelve to sixteen feet lip to lip. I returned and with the aid of the officers handled the companies to their places in some kind of packed formation.

'If the Germans were to start shelling!'

There was no need to look for trouble. They did not. By extraordinary luck I stumbled on an orderly who led me to the brigade HQ. The conclave was over. There remained only to issue a few boxes of rockets and Verey lights (star lights) to the already loaded men. The ground was a slippery sea of mud. The rain was becoming torrential. Owing to a mischance, we stood for over an hour waiting for our guides. Imagine the nightmare! At last the signal to move off was given. My work was done. I had handed the battalion over to the CO and my orders were to return to the reserve of officers and NCOs at the transport bivouac. I stood as the men, cursing cheerfully, filed past. They were going forward to what? A dry bed at any rate awaited me. Those others were going through mud to a homeless goal, wet, tired, under shellfire, nearing the enemy. I wished them luck and turned to mount my dripping mare for the homeward journey.

On the night of 4/5 September, the battalion entered the Valley of Death. There was no hostile shelling as the long line of men picked its way through Bernafay Wood and Trônes Wood—but it was raining as it always did during a major offensive. The battlefield was a mass of water-filled craters and littered with the debris of the fighting which had taken place there over the past few days. Everywhere could be seen shreds of uniform and equipment, perforated helmets, broken stretchers, broken rifles and boots, not quite empty. The sight of this hell was enough to cause any man to quiver as they passed by on their way to a similar fate.

The wounded had all been removed, but the dead lay there stiff and stark, with open staring eyes, just as they had fallen. Some lay as if they were sleeping quietly, others had died in agony—the contents of their haversacks scattered around. Khaki and grey-clad forms were intermingled. Legs doubled together, heads askew. Heads, trunks and limbs from former battles trampled underfoot emitting a frightful stench.

These images are drawn mainly from Father Willie Doyle's writings, but even the official history, which is for the most part impassive, was moved to tell of shapeless masses of human beings lying strewn over the ground and the air reeking with the smell of half-rotten corpses. As others have observed, dead Germans smelled different to British dead and retained their fierce countenance. The colour of dead faces changed from white to grey, to red, to purple to green, to black and then to slimy.

Perhaps the most graphic account of this nightmare march is that of Willie Doyle. But characteristically, it is also compassionate. In the bottom of one hole he saw a British and a German soldier, locked in a deadly embrace, neither had any weapon, but they had fought on to the bitter end. Another two seemed to have died hand-in-hand praying for and forgiving one another. One corpse clutched at what had been a mortal wound, a young boy lay there calm and peaceful, with a smile of happiness on his face, as if he had had a glimpse of heaven before he died. Another had an expression of infinite sadness as if in a lucid moment before death there came a thought of home.

For now Alex was spared the horrors of Death Valley, as he had parted company with the rest of the battalion. Being left out of battle, he headed back the way he had come, believing that his job was done. The story of his own small role in the great Battle of Guillemont continues with his return to 'B' Echelon:

To Maricourt, was easy going. After Maricourt, I found the road blocked. A string of carts travelling east on the right hand side of the road, a string of carts travelling west on the left. In the centre, French infantry in file snaked through the other way. Here and there, a halted horseman, cap peak like water spout, felt for a passage. A subaltern stood with motor broken down and half drawn across the road. Slowly, methodically, I gained forward moves through the crush, not without small penalties, a muttered curse from a foot-slogger banged, a knock on the knee from a cart. It was a dream, bodily discomfort passed. Detached wonder only at the scene remained. At last with a great creaking, something seemed to give, and soon the whole roadway was grinding into motion like some huge rumbling machinery.

I reached the camp at 4.00 a.m., stumbled over tent ropes, and roused a sleeping orderly with a lamp. Assuring myself that he was most concerned about the horse, I found my tent, ate three Jacobs biscuits, stripped off my dripping clothes, left them in a sodden pyramid on the floor of the tent, got into dry pyjamas, and with a sudden glow of warmth into my sleeping bag and knew no more until nine o'clock next morning.

It had taken the troops twelve hours to get from Billon Farm to their positions where they relieved what was left of the 12th Rifle Brigade at 5.30 a.m. on 5 September. The relief had been carried out without casualties but later in the day, casualties started to mount from shelling. This corner of the Somme battlefield was deceptively small. Longuval,

Guillemont and Ginchy make a triangle with each side being about 1,500 yards long. Leuze Wood in turn, is about 1,500 yards from the Guillemont—Ginchy side of the triangle. Combles lies in a hollow behind Leuze Wood. The 48th and 49th brigades were straddling a railway line between the Ginchy—Guillemont line and Leuze Wood. At B Echelon HQ, Alex was itching to get forward:

Next morning things appeared more normal. But existence seemed empty and useless hanging about camp so far in the rear with no news of the battalion. I set the men to work building rain-proof shelters and then made my preparations to start for the firing line. I got the cook to roast some beef, packed up biscuits, a tin of fruit salad which had arrived opportunely from England, whisky and a bottle of champagne, one of half a dozen that the HQ mess had bought for special occasions. With this good cheer stowed away in a sand-bag, I started off with Treanor, my orderly, and a map, on foot. The weather was fine and dull, and soon settled down again into the endless drizzle. However, it was pleasant walking. We reached Maricourt—a quiet orchard-draped smiling village in times of peace. Ample solid built houses and out buildings enclosing the central dung heap and sewer pond lined the shady streets. Now they stood, burst, roofless, and shell-torn, a melancholy sight.

Once more we took the road to the *Briqueterie* [a gutted brick factory about 250 yards south of Bernafay Wood]. I swung to the right and made for the village of Hardecourt two miles away. With constant reference to a map which soon became pulp in the rain, I plugged along followed by the faithful Treanor, the sack on his back. The country was not altogether deserted. Out of the heavy mist two khaki figures would cut across my path and pass out of sight. On a ridge to the right or left, ones and twos would show a blurred outline and disappear. And always beyond, encircling my forward march, fell the boom and crash of heavy shells, muffled seemingly in the writhing mist.

I called a halt at the dug-out of a spruce French officer of artillery who gave me a genial nod and on my enquiring the road, took me into the dry and turned over many maps telling me volubly the road to follow and more important, what a map cannot do—the roads to avoid. I could not stay long. Already the afternoon was drawing on and only half the journey done. We parted with mutual expressions of cordiality and good faith in the Allies cause.

I passed now through groups of French guns at work for I was behind the French lines at Combles—the juncture of the British and the French. The men looked at me curiously and one made a friendly remark. On we went to Hardicourt, another shattered village, up the winding narrow street and still saw no mark by which I could identify my goal. All marks familiar in a countryside had vanished.

It was now that I went wrong and lost myself in the front line of battle. I must have taken a road out of Hardicourt exactly at right angles to the road I should have taken. Presently I found myself skirting a hill, the boundary of a gulley on the other side of which rose a precipitous wooden ridge, which I identified on my sodden map as Savernake. [Savernake Wood is a small plantation south of Combles]. In front of me were lines of blue-coated infantry—French evidently preparing to advance. I wandered among them, lost. Fresh-faced boy subalterns rushed up to me jubilant, and plied me with questions.

'Has Combles fallen?' (Combles did not fall till a fortnight later).

'The Bosches are on the run.'

'Nous les avons donnés une pille' was their expression. 'We have given them the knock.'

'See, the artillery is going forward.'

I looked back over my left shoulder and on the hillside I had just left saw guns and their limbers coming up at the gallop, wheeling into position and firing—the famous seventy-fives.

'Where are the British?' I asked.

'Ah, les Anglais. Look, they are on that hill to your right.'

Sure enough, I looked and saw the familiar khaki swarming. I was very much out of my road. Here was where khaki and blue joined, the exact geographical spot in all this weltering line. It was a puzzling country. Smooth, rounded hills dipped into valleys deep and shallow, narrow and wide—a fall and we could see no more than the hollow in which one stood, a rise and the wreckage of copses, all of whose names are now familiar.

I faced about and fearing the approach of twilight hurried over the uneven ground, here a pastured vale rising to stubble, there the level of a twisted railway creeping on a hill foot, a blob of cars overturned, abandoned, a broken toy. A French soldier waved me back and pointed. I bent my path to his gesticulation and always at my heels, dogged the faithful Treanor, the interval between us increasing as the pace and hard going began to tell.

Up a sunken road I crept, lane only by line of bank, hedge no more. To my left on the high ground a major, le commandant stood with his glasses glued to his eyes watching the distant ridge. At last, climbing, I reached an extensive plateau and there saw some 300 yards ahead the familiar line of flat caps. A few figures stood silhouetted against the skyline. Officers! I approached the group. They were the CO of an English battalion and his staff. Question and answer followed.

'I want to get to Guillemont,' I said.

'That's Guillemont there. Over there is Falfemont Farm' he replied.

That Guillemont! I thought as I followed his finger along the skyline and saw no more than a nipple on the even line of dark against the grey. A scattered company of broken trees lay along the hillside, noticeable even at that distance for their ruin. Worse than any blackened derelicts of a forest fire that shows tortured, naked limbs, rigid in impotent dumb protest to heaven—that, the work of natural agency, but this more loathsome the work of man. Houses? None. The British shells had done their work thoroughly. Just as a garden roller will flatten out a colony of worm casts or leave smooth the site of a mole hill, so had the village of Guillemont been blotted out. In a few seconds, these thoughts had flashed through my mind.

'That point?' I said.

'All that shows of the cemetery of Guillemont,' was the answer.

'You had better keep round that high point to your left, if you cross the dip you will run into heavy shelling: besides, it is exposed to view of the German lines.'

I turned again and made off; and now I came to the ground where there was not a yard unplastered with shells, pitted like the surface of the moon in photographs. The only path ran circling round the contingent edges of the craters. Some giant hand had shaken the surface soil and rained the friable clods evenly around. The going was hard. It was getting dark. I had not yet found the battalion. My orderly was lagging. Constantly, I had to wait, schooling my patience. Poor devil! He was carrying a load and his rifle; I—a haversack containing six bottles of soda. I waited for him and took his rifle—he protesting. On, we must push on. For all I know of the land, we may wonder through our as yet unlinked lines, or worse, stumble unawares, unrecognized on our own sentries.

'What is that?' A figure lay half concealed behind a ruck of earth, rifle to shoulder, pointing dead at us. Little round cap, colour blue grey in the failing light. I felt for my revolver. Fool! It had worked round the centre of my back. Two minutes to get it out now, besides it always jambs in this rotten holster. To be shot like this alone, no friends near, and to no purpose. We dropped together and we crawled in a semi-circle. A careful view over a shell hole. Ah! The figure never moved. Dead! Shot at the game the day before. Fallen in a natural attitude, it still appeared to hold the line, but now stiff and blue with white fingers crooked about his rifle.

'Come on' I shouted. And now we passed groups of dead bodies, British and German huddled together in the unmistakable attitude of the lifeless. At last an empty jam tin on a crooked stick was sighted. A mark!

We made for it. Heads were seen crowded in a trench.

'Our own people' I cried, and ran forward leaving Treanor to follow. Yes it was dark, but we were home.

Alex arrived on the evening of the 5th to find the battalion HQ in a derelict enemy shelter south of Guillemont village. The battalion was spread out in a semi-circle, poised to attack Leuze Wood (commonly known as Lousey Wood). The disposition of the companies at this time was as follows:

'A' Company (Captain V. H. Parr) on the west side of Leuze Wood.

'B' Company (Captain R.G. Kerr) and 'D' Coy in a shell crater position along the Ginchy—Wedge Wood road. (Wedge Wood no longer exists and neither does the railway line).

'C' Company (Captain J. Ritty) on the Guillemont—Leuze Wood road.

In Alex's absence during the day, there had been some shelling and Captain Stainforth, the commander of 'D' Company had been wounded in the leg and evacuated but casualties were light. Some patrols probed the woods but otherwise the night was uneventful. During the night, Harry brought up rations and ammunition in a jolting, clattering, convoy of wagons and limbers but could get his wagons no further than Maltz Horn Farm. Jingling nerves of the drivers were calmed by the reassuring gentleness of the mules.

By the time the Irish Brigade joined the battle, Guillemont itself had been captured and the next objectives were Leuze Wood, east of the town, and Ginchy to the north. Alex had taken it upon himself to come up to Battalion HQ from the reserve area without orders but his presence was appreciated, not least because of the whiskey which he produced from his pack:

The CO was glad to see me and told me all the battalion's adventures since we parted. We went off together to visit the companies pushed forward towards the enemy's line. Leuze wood had recently been taken by our troops, and the battalion held the south west corner and along a sunken road towards Ginchy. The headquarters and two companies were in a trench south of Guillemont, across the valley from and facing Leuze Wood.

That night, or what was left of it, I spent in a German dug out with eleven others. The HQ of the 8th Battalion shared its shelter. There were two stories. The first, 12 feet below ground was merely a passage at right angles to the steps which cut the centre. This passage was 14 feet long and four broad with an 'L' shaped bend at one end forming a small chamber. The steps continued down to another shelter ten foot lower which I never visited. A few odd shelves at an awkward angle tilting forward, a broken chair and some empty boxes were all the furnishings. The floor was littered with old coats, sacks and bits of German equipment cemented with mud. Two flickering candles relieved the gloom.

Many people came and went. A telephone was fixed at the bottom step, and gave out a continuous buzz as messages came in. We made a lordly supper off cold beef and biscuits and fruit salad from a tin and then retired to sleep for a few hours, ready to tumble out at any alarm.

I sat on a step with my feet resting on steps above. By my right hand was a white sleeping face. By 5.00 a.m. I was awake and had a feeling of repulsion for the tomb-like dug-out. I crawled up the steps and found that dawn had broken. The rain clouds had passed leaving a clear sky. A warm gentle wind was blowing. It was good to be alive for one more morning in the promise of a glorious September day. But though the sky was fresh and clean, around me lay the muck of battle, the ruined land, the blasted trees; and ever and anon, a faint smell of corruption mingled with the air, and tantalized the nostrils. The runners and police of headquarters were already on the move seeking warmth by movement after a chilly night, hands in pockets, collars up to ears, with muddy coats and smeared but cheerful faces.

I paid a visit to the two companies in the trench overlooking Leuze Wood. The trench which followed the line of the sunken road, though no road could be imagined, looked square on Leuze Wood and the hog-back running south parallel to our trench across the valley from it. Close under Leuze Wood the valley reached a dead end, blocked by high ground north of Ginchy and shown on the map by the 150 metre contour which circled the telegraph pole, the highest point. Behind, lay the site of Guillemont already described, the only mark a leaning cross girt about by a twisted ornamental wire fence.

After a chat with the officers, I returned, and had great difficulty in finding headquarters. I met the colonel at the entrance to the dug-out. Together we went off across the head of the valley to visit the company in the neighbourhood of Leuze Wood. We found them in two narrow half-dug ditches facing the high ground north of Ginchy, and slightly below it. But from the south west corner of the wood, a good view could be obtained right across this high ground up to Ginchy itself. In this spot, the company headquarters had been established. A concrete machine gun emplacement of the Germans had been crippled for use of machine gun but undamaged as a shelter. Besides, it was a perfect dug-out with bunks, table, chairs and other furnishings. It was a position of great strength for the Germans, yet abandoned by them without a blow being exchanged in our impetuous dash on Leuze Wood.

The CO, his orders in hand, asked me to assist in the disposition of a second company in the forward line and then departed to examine our left. The company I awaited soon began to come up in extended order and had to pass over ground exposed to view and fire from the high ground north of Ginchy. The Germans kept firing pairs of red lights, which I guessed to be a signal to their artillery. I met the company commander and asked him to move his men up more quickly under cover of the dead ground and a sunken road, and to leave one of his machine guns to sweep the line of enemy trench that was giving trouble and make the occupants keep their heads down. Then for two hours, I lay in the corner of Leuze wood with my glasses watching the movements of the Germans. My corner was marked; every now and then, a 4.2' would crash through the trees and burst in the soft earth, splattering me with mud. Fortunately, the shells were falling short. Meanwhile, considerable activity was apparent on the German side. Figures of many men came running up and disappeared in a trench which must have been some 300 to 400 yards away. Either the enemy were preparing a local counter-attack or feared one. The company commander was at my side.

'Get a Lewis gun to this corner', I said, 'the cover is good and the field of fire excellent'.

The order went out. After some delay, two machine gunners came running. Bullets splashed around them as they ran. They won through unhurt ending up among the tangle of undergrowth and worked at fixing the gun. More delay.

'Why don't you open fire?'

'Sir she's jammed, a bullet hit her crossing the open, Look!'

It was true, there was a big dent where a bullet had struck the gun in a vital part. The gun was useless but had saved the man who carried it. Soon after, the unit on our right brought up a gun, and opened fire with good effect.

At this time, nearly the whole of Ginchy was in our possession. I watched the two lines of starlight, feeble in the bright sunshine, our own and the Germans', that marked the most forward lines of each for the aeroplanes which circled over us at stated hours to alter the map to our advance for the information of the gunners. But now away on our left, I saw extended lines of men, rising, running forward, and eating their way into our line by the eastern boundary of Ginchy. A bombing fight was in progress in which the Germans succeeded in driving our troops back, and, I learnt later, retook Ginchy.

I spent two hours in this place sending back messages to headquarters. Later when the battalion became quiet I determined to return myself. It was no easy matter. The exit from the wood was exposed, and the enemy were on the watch. Shells were bursting in the valley without apparent system, such that one could find a lane between the beaten areas. As I left the wood, I heard the zip-zip of bullets striking the ground about my feet, throwing up little points of dirt. I had been spotted. Throwing dignity to the winds, I threw myself into a shell hole. Bullets whistled past my ears. A brief halt and then dashes from shell hole to shell hole. At length, I drew out to blind ground and could walk at my leisure. Now there was only danger from bursting shells. After all, what man, if he has time to think at all does not reckon his chances and put them at 1000 to 1 against being hit. One gets to despise the shells but hates the noise; and even the terrifying explosions of many shells appear something less dreadful than the brutal bark of a machine gun, that will sweep down hundreds in a minute.

I watched a little figure on the steep slope opposite staggering under a sandbag full of rations or some such load. He looked so small and less than human in the sweep of country as he crept along with an uneven gait. Big shells were bursting to his left. Nearer they came and nearer. He kept his way unheeding, circling the holes in his path with the erratic stagger of a cinematograph. Sixty yards—forty yards—twenty yards and then it happened! My heart pounded, a fountain of earth sprang at his feet. His form leant for a second, against the uprising, outspreading cone of dirt. A second more, he was gone from sight. Extraordinary miracle! He rose again at one and staggered on his way, with his load, unhurt, unheeding, appearing to treat the burst of a six inch shell as some ordinary phenomenon of life, unconnected with the work he had in hand.

I ran into two companies in extended lines making their way forward along the hollow. What masses of men we had in reserve behind the battle outposts, flung far out to keep in touch with the enemy. But surely, they were on our sector of the front.

'Who are you?'

'The _____ Fusiliers'.

'Ah yes, the battalion on our left. You are a bit out of your way, what are your orders?'

'Yes, bear a little to your left and make for that line of trees. You will find a company there, get in touch with them, and keep going along the low ground to get some cover.'

The battalion headquarters was again most difficult to find in that dreary waste. I wandered for some time before I chanced upon the spot.

'The CO is badly wounded and gone down. You are in command'.

'That is bad. Where is the adjutant?'

'In the dug-out at the telephone?'

Messages were coming in from the brigade.

'You are to prepare to attack the position in front of Ginchy. The hour will be notified later'.

News spread quickly that Colonel Oxo Young had been wounded quite early on the 6th while visiting Captain Kerr and 'B' Company. He had been shot by a sniper and was not expected to live. It was a crucial stage of the battle and it was indeed fortuitous that Alex had come up for a visit the night before. This was the first time that he was acting as battalion commander and he was immediately put to the test.

By now, the Germans had given up part of Leuze Wood but then some troops from a different battalion (not of the Irish Division) broke and ran and there were reports that the enemy had captured the wood and the HQ was threatened. In the night, a hurricane of shell fire descended on the whole of the battalion area while machine guns raked their flank from the direction of Ginchy. This turned out to be a prelude to an infantry counter-attack. But with the artillery support, Captain Parr managed to rally men of different units and repulsed the attack then led his own counter-attack and ended up in control of the whole of Leuze Wood. The entire episode lasted forty-five minutes. For these actions, Parr was awarded the Military Cross.

This Battle of Guillemont has become legendary in the annals of Irish military history, and Alex played a leading role during his short tenure as commanding officer. Few other observers of this piece of the action would have had such a thorough appreciation of the battlefield combined with his descriptive powers:

Messages had to be sent out to the companies. Later this order was cancelled owing to Ginchy being again in the hands of the Germans and our left exposed. The day was spent receiving and answering messages, arranging parties to carry up rations. When darkness fell, the comparative quiet of occasional shell and machine gun fire began to grow in volume and soon became a terrifying roar of sound. One had to shout to be heard.

An attack! The headquarters company to stand to. Message flashed from the brigade. Report awaited from the front company. Two miserable creatures from another unit were brought in. Their nerves were gone.

'The Germans are attacking Leuze Wood in force' was their cry. 'Our men are pouring back along the ridge'.

Still no message from the front company. This story cannot be true—the exaggeration of unhinged minds.

'How is it you are the only two arrived?'

No answer to that.

'Confine these men for spreading alarm and despondency and hand them over to their own unit as soon as opportunity offers.'

All this in the appalling din. I shall go up to the reserve companies and see Captain_____. He may have news. A guide took me up through the darkness lit by the blinding flashes of the shells which only served to make the returning darkness felt. Captain _____ was optimistic.

'I see nothing to cause alarm. There is a heavy barrage between us and the wood.'

'When it lifts, send up two platoons in case they want reinforcements. Nothing can live in that storm.'

At last the message which will help to clear the situation arrives.

'The Germans have attacked Leuze Wood, and gained an entry in the north west corner. Our men are holding their ground.'

A later message told me that the troops on the right had counter-attacked and driven the Germans out and beyond the wood. Our artillery was now thundering in answer, and continued to lash the threatened corner long after the German guns had frittered out to silence. So impetuous had been our counter-attack that a platoon of _____ Fusiliers had gone beyond the wood and come under our own gun fire. Lieutenant _____ was killed by the burst of our own shell. Lieutenant _____ a smart young L/G officer engaged six Germans single handed, killed five and was bayoneted in the chest and killed by the sixth.

The unflappable Captain Parr was wounded during the assault but remained on duty. When the situation had stabilized, Alex ordered 'B' and 'D' companies forward for close support in case the Boche renewed his attack at dawn. At the same time, he moved his headquarters forward to that evacuated by 'D' Company to reduce the distance over which runners had to carry messages:

What of the runners that bear the messages through the barrages? Suddenly a figure starts up in the darkness, rifle slung on shoulder, and hands in a slip of paper. The answer is written and he vanishes as he came. Splendid boys, some of them no more than seventeen years old, they consider nothing but the slip of paper that has been entrusted to them, and its destination, having a wonderful instinctive knowledge of their way. Well had been the COs selection and training been justified. One young fellow with the face of a girl had taken a message to the front and was given another to take back. Soon after, he was shot in the arm, but transferred the message to his other hand and went on. His other arm was hit. He was found lying in a shell hole some yards from his goal with the message between his teeth and another wound in his head. He was carried in and sent down. His wounds were not serious and he recovered.

After the row, came quiet but there was to be no rest that night. New dispositions of the companies had to be made during the hours of darkness. Our line was to be pushed further forward, feeling its way nearer the enemy. HQ had to be advanced, to keep in touch, leaving the security of the dug-out for an open trench.

I made a tour of the outpost line to see that all was well and arrange for the new movements. The guide that had led me lost the way in the dark. Stumbling about in a maze of broken trenches I lost all sense of direction. The stars were obscured. A shadowy group of figures filed towards me. Were they our men? A low challenge brought a British response. They located my whereabouts and eventually I reached Leuze Wood. Capt Parr gave me a full account of the happenings in the wood during the early part of the night. He had been touched in the neck by a fragment of shell. I insisted on him returning with me to have the wound properly dressed at the battalion aid post. We started, I'm in front, then he. Then two Tommies of the _____ with a prisoner between them that they would not let out of reach at any price. They had lost their battalion and attached themselves to our party. Two orderlies brought up the rear—a queer procession filing down. The prisoner blinked in the blaze of an electric torch. He was very quiet, dazed but hopeful. No doubt at heart he was not sorry to be safe although on the wrong side of the line.

It was nearly daybreak when I reached headquarters. I lay down on the fire step and got two hours sleep. Next morning was again fine. I set the men to improving our home. Picks and shovels and material were lying about broadcast. The trench was to be deepened, shelters begun. After breakfast, I was seated on the parapet above the trench. There was a sudden explosion. A blow as from a club struck me in the right eye. The world turned warm and rosy red with a smell of crushed flowers.

'Is this the end?'

I put my hand to my face. The blood poured down my nose onto my sleeve. I heard a voice say,

'The Major is hit'. And someone ran forward to bind the wound.

'I think my eye is gone' I said. 'But otherwise I seem to be alive.'

With the wound thoroughly dressed, I walked to see what damage had been done to the others. But a cold shiver of weakness settled down my spine and I had to sit down. My faithful orderly ran up and gave me his arm to the dressing station. The doctor examined the wound.

'Your eye is saved' he said, 'a nasty blow on the eyebrow. You will soon be right again.'

So my eye was not gone, but I was out of it all after only two or three days. Back along the road we had all travelled so recently I was to go, while the others remained to see more severe fighting, harder times and heavier casualties than we had yet had. A group of wounded were collected and sent down to the nearest advanced field dressing station. It was a long tramp. The shells still burst around us, and now the odds against being hit had diminished. How could any man escape? Would we never be out of their reach? And now scenes shifted rapidly. Back to the field dressing station among groups of wounded. Inside the shelter lay the bad cases, bloody, bandaged heaps among which the doctors moved, swiftly adjusting, deftly binding. Back along the road to Maricourt, every little jolt now a purgatory. Back the straight long pave lined with poplars. Back to the casualty clearing station, where a short halt was made until the hospital train was ready. The sound of war grew dim and died away. Back smoothly gliding to Rouen. Back softly rocking on the hospital ship. BACK- BACK- TO BLIGHTY. [Capitals by A. D. Reid].

The shell which delivered Alex's 'Blighty one' on the morning of the 7th had also hit RSM Dolan and three other headquarters personnel. The only staff still standing at headquarters were Second Lieutenant Foley, the signals officer, and Lieutenant G. A. C. Walker who in 1920 brought out the official history. Three out of the four company commanders were casualties. Captains V. Parr and C. Stainforth, were wounded. Captain J. Ritty was first reported missing on 9 September, and death was finally accepted many weeks later. He had only been back with his company for a month after recovering from being badly gassed on 27 April, at which time he had won the MC for conspicuous gallantry. One of the originals from Ireland, Ritty had been a fine athlete. Colonel Young wrote to Mr and Mrs Ritty at their home in Harbour View, Sligo, about their son, Jack's, sterling value as a soldier. 'His loss is not only yours, but of everyone in the battalion whose name he had so splendidly helped to make.'

Captain R. G. Kerr now took over command of the 7th Battalion. Harry had to carry on as usual, but at least his work in bringing up a substantial ration of rum to the men in the trenches was much appreciated. On the call of 'roll up for your rum', each man brought his favourite vessel and the precious liquid was fairly distributed.

The work of the 16th (Irish) Division in the Battle of Guillemont was not yet finished. Their most impressive feat was the attack on Ginchy on 9 September. The 49th Brigade was in support. The whistle sounded at four o'clock and the men of the 47th and 48th brigades ran or walked, in broken array, in and out of shell holes and along the narrow ledges that separated them. In just eight minutes, the wild rush of the Irish swept through Ginchy. Supporting artillery shelled the rear of the village keeping German reinforcements from arriving while the cellars in town were cleared.

According to one onlooker, the Irishmen would have been in Berlin had the officers not frantically blown their whistles, shouted and gesticulated to stop them. The glory of it all was intoxicating. In 1918, before the war had ended, Arthur Conan Doyle brought out a history of the Somme battles. With his flair for the superlative, he wrote of how the Irish 'stormers' inspired even the British riflemen with their Celtic yells blended with the scream of their pipes. Bodies and limbs were thrown into the air yet no man faltered.

Unfair though it may be to single out a few individuals for their actions, one could mention the 'boy hero of Ginchy', the eighteen year old Second Lieutenant James Dalton of the Dublin Fusiliers who took command of two companies and led them to their objective—then held that position against all odds. Likewise, when two senior commanders became casualties, Second Lieutenant Hugh Abbott Green of the Royal Inniskilling Fusiliers took control of two companies, and although wounded, advanced eighty yards and consolidated his position. Both were awarded the Military Cross, and Green later got a bar to his MC.

The story of the 16th (Irish) Division at Ginchy would not be complete without mentioning the death in action of Lieutenant Tom Kettle the Irish poet, barrister, journalist, academic and politician. After just 52 days with the 9th Royal Dublin Fusiliers, this man of many talents was killed at the head of his company during the attack on the afternoon of 9 September. A bullet, or shell splinter, penetrated above the steel waistcoat he was wearing. An officer named Boyd collected Lieutenant Kettle's papers from his body but then he himself, together with the papers, was blown to atoms. At the time of his death, Kettle was writing a book about the division and the war. Mrs Mary Kettle launched a crusade to discover the whereabouts of her husband's body, but inevitably no trace was found. Tom Kettle's most famous poem which was written for his daughter and begins 'In wiser days my darling rosebud blown...' was found on a scrap of paper marked: 'Betty. In the field before Guillemont. September 4th 1916.'

Officers, who were identified by their uniforms, were especially targeted and Colonel Dalzell Walton CO of the 8th Inniskillings was shot and killed by a sniper shortly before the attack. His successor would also not survive the war. Within the 16th Division as a whole, five battalion commanders were casualties. A story which is attributed to the colonel of an Irish regiment is therefore ironic. At the Battle of Guillemont, the colonel noticed that a private was following him everywhere—especially where the fighting was the heaviest. The colonel thought that perhaps the private was anxious for his well-being but the private later explained: 'My mother says to me, Sor, "Stick to the colonel, and you'll be all right. Them colonels never get hurt".'

Even in its role as the support battalion, the 7th Inniskillings suffered heavily. No less than four subalterns were killed in the attack. Total casualties were five officers and 184 other ranks. Although worse battles lay ahead, this surpassed anything the battalion had experienced before. In the words of Arthur Conan Doyle, it seemed 'beyond the general scheme of human experience'.

After the successful capture of Ginchy, the battalion was withdrawn from the line and moved to the rear—to the pleasant town of Bailleul. A piper played old Irish rhapsodies—a blending of joy and grief. Lamenting and yearning, belligerent and challenging, the music expresses the melancholy and mysticism of the Irish.

The camp fires were burning low when the grinding column made its way back. First came the field guns with horsemen nodding off in their saddles, followed by wagons and field kitchens. Then came the infantry, limping and shuffling along. Mounted officers rode in their sleep, only the occasional word was muttered. Immediately, the officers set about reorganizing the depleted companies and platoons.

It took ten hours for the wounded to travel the sixty miles by hospital train from Corbie to Rouen. There was an atmosphere of pain and sorrow on that train. Men were dying on it. The horrors which they had escaped from still remained vivid and cruel. Alex felt only relief knowing that he was not close to death and had not lost a limb. The pleasing thing about being wounded was that responsibility was taken away from you and you became somebody else's problem. Someone described it as 'travelling like a parcel' taken out at appropriate places.

Like the legions of wounded from the Somme battles who had travelled this path, Alex was admitted to hospital at Rouen. There were more than ten Commonwealth hospitals on the southern outskirts of the city, mostly in the vicinity of the racecourse. The city was conveniently situated for a staging area being close to Le Havre. Within a few days, Margaret Reid received a telegram stating that her son had been slightly wounded but only on 18 September did his name appear on the wounded list in the *Morning Post*. Even for a high ranking officer, a 'Blighty' was a much prized ticket home. Being a superficial wound, it was patched up all too soon, but Alex was granted a full two months convalescence leave which allowed him the opportunity to travel to Canada and see his mother one last time.

For those like Harry who survived the Battle of the Somme without so much as a scratch, there was no respite. The battalion was loaded onto buses and trains and moved north through Normandy, Hazebrouck and St Jean Cappel into Belgium. On 23 September they relieved the 33rd Canadian Infantry in the Spanbroekmolen sector about one and a half miles east of Kemmel Hill. Fortunately, it was a quiet sector but defences were not ideal and the great unseen were disapproving of 'stagnation trench warfare'. There appeared to be an unspoken 'live and let live' arrangement in place but the Irish soon 'put the wind up the Hun' with regular artillery bombardments and patrolling of no man's land. Days grew shorter and colder putting an end to any major operations. With this pause came the happy news that home leave was to be allowed.

CHAPTER 8

To Blighty and back to Belgium

Autumn came and went, and melancholy set in with the November cold. Only home leave could pick up the morale of the troops. Officers were given leave every eight months or so. After a particularly hard time in the line, this period could be shortened. Almost all the NCO's and men who had come out with the battalion, the old originals, were granted leave to England and Ireland at the end of 1916. Sadly, as it transpired, some may have been overlooked.

London was still essentially London, and this fact was inclined to shock a man who had just returned from a slaughterhouse. The contrast was just too much to digest. It seemed that there were two distinct societies in England, and the most visible one made a mockery of what was happening on the front. Then there were those who had lost sons and husbands and had lost their focus in life. They tended to withdraw into themselves and went unnoticed. Fighting men were held in high esteem, every newspaper and magazine sang their praise. The unsung heroes were the women who waited and worried.

It was a time of terrible food shortages owing to the German submarine blockade. People had to queue for any imported goods. Meat, butter and sugar were strictly rationed but the rich businessmen in their clubs still managed to feast on ham, turkey and chicken. Apparently the best food in London was served upstairs at the Café Royal. Taxi drivers profiteered from shortages of fuel and were hated for it. Conversation seemed to mainly revolve around the shortages of coal and food. But money could buy anything.

Those who could afford it, coped by drinking hard and living a life of self-indulgence. Bars were supposed to stop serving liquor by 10.00 p.m. but patrons got around it by drinking whisky out of coffee mugs. Soho was in its heyday with more than 200 disreputable clubs and the commensurate number of ladies of ill repute. New dances had emerged to go with the Ragtime music. Out went the 'Foxtrot' and in came the 'Grisly Bear'. Music halls and restaurants did lively business with soldiers home on leave.

The theatre was also having a good year and the musical comedy *Chu Chin Chow* had just opened at His Majesty's Theatre and was to run for another five years. The play 'Belinda', by A. A. Milne was showing at a private venue. It was apparently light and whimsical but quite entertaining. At the Alhambra, *The Bing Boys are Here* was a revue not to be missed by the young and energetic crowd. It was a portrayal of London life which produced the most renowned song of the day, 'If you were the only girl in the world' and many others including 'Another little drink wouldn't do us any harm'—which seemed to be the prevailing philosophy.

In the midst of this, the wounded and maimed were walking reminders that there was a war on. Casualty lists appeared day after day adding to the collective grief. By 1917, almost every family had been touched by death. Bombing raids also brought the war home—to the point that Londoners were inclined to think that they were bearing the brunt of the war.

London residents were awed by the great airships which periodically floated over on their bombing raids. On 1 October 1916, a zeppelin was shot down over north London, falling like a burning paper bag, roasting its human contents. For civilians, it was mere theatre, like the rest of the war. Newspapers were blamed for this disconnect with reality. Actual warfare was vicariously experienced by the readers. Newspapers published the work of soldier poets (mostly bad). Diaries, memoirs and letters home were often serialized and read with interest. The *Morning Post* was a bellicose, pro-war paper which attempted to convince readers that the dead were gloriously happy. The papers were fond of printing the last letters from young officers which were apt to state that they had really felt happy to die—as though going over the top was a sort of religious experience.

New Year's Eve was a sombre occasion, there were no wild parties and celebrations. At breakfast on 1 January 1917, the public were greeted with newspaper reports expressing grim resolve to carry on until ultimate victory—regardless of cost. There was a rising anti-war sentiment but censorship was ruthlessly enforced.

Wounded soldiers in hospitals tended towards self-pity and estrangement. At their bedsides, visitors would try to avoid all talk of the war. Soldiers were carrying something in their heads which belonged to them alone. Worried relatives would rush to hospitals all over England and sometimes even to France to ascertain for themselves the seriousness of an injury.

Allowing for six weeks in hospital and altogether three weeks of traveling by boat and by train, Alex was still able to spend a month in Canada, with a few days left over to attend to business in London. At the divisional depot at Woking, he was pronounced fit by a Medical Board consisting of grey-haired army doctors who seemed more concerned with the paperwork than with medical matters. That it was Christmas time mattered not at all to the army, and without further fuss, Alex was for it again.

Returning to the front was a depressing prospect—especially over the festive season which coincided with a bitterly cold spell. At Waterloo station, one was visibly reminded of how hard this war was on one's family, even though they were incapable of understanding the front line experience. Mothers accompanied their sons with a mixture of pride and wretchedness. The scene was at once depressing, inspiring and historical. Fresh troops entraining in their crisp new uniforms among twenty year old veterans with hunched shoulders, reluctantly returning from leave. Porters went about their work. With heart-breaking mirth, boyish laughter resounded from the carriages. A thousand dramas were played out daily, personified by lingering kisses and last glances. Women broke down and sobbed when the guard blew his piercing whistle and the doom-laden train disappeared from sight.

At the various stations en route to Southampton, soldiers who had not packed their own provisions purchased refreshments from boys carrying wicker baskets. The racks were loaded with bulging parcels, held together by string. Officers sat in separate carriages where they read newspapers and were served a respectable lunch. Conversation typically revolved around the cause of the war and the prospect of its finish. Serious talk intermingled with light-hearted banter about the benefits of obtaining a 'blighty'.

All army luggage looked alike, and in England there was no system for the orderly transportation thereof. On arrival at the terminus, it was simply thrown out of the carriage into a heap and one had to fight to extricate it from the scramble. Porters stood ready at the docks to load the baggage and although they were now dressed in military uniform, they were not above soliciting a tip through subtle gestures and expressions. At one juncture, Alex's luggage was mislaid—much to his consternation, because to miss the boat to Le Havre would mean a certain court martial.

Crossing the English Channel, one was aware only of the grey waves and the imminence of France. Havre was a glitter of lights on dark water. From here, it was a gentle 70 mile journey up the river Seine to Rouen— seven hours of interesting landscape and architecture. The bells of Rouen floated on the morning air heralding one's arrival.

Rouen is an historic city where Joan of Arc was burned at the stake, but during the war it held little cultural appeal. It was a place where people showed no interest in each other because they were only passing through. A list was posted on the notice board with the names of those who were going up the line the next day. Men crowded around with feigned nonchalance. On the same board was a list of men sentenced to be executed for cowardice. The sordid brothels in Rouen were well patronized by youngsters who did not want to die virgins. On the positive side, the Drapeau Blanc, a house of ill repute, saved the lives of many a young boy who ended up in venereal hospitals being no use for trench service. Little boys accosted soldiers in the street, soliciting for their alleged sisters, 'very good jig-a-jig'. The charge was ten francs, and afterwards, there was much discussion of the bed-manners of Frenchwomen.

Had Alex been permitted a longer stopover in Rouen, he could have had a bath and dinner at the Hôtel de la Post which apparently served the best meals in town. The hotel had become a sort of club, frequented by every British officer employed in the vicinity. Those particular about their toilette came for a haircut, shave, shampoo and face massage. Rambling around Rouen pretending to be a peacetime tourist, one could peep in at a service in the cathedral or walk the narrow streets of the old quarter, window shopping and exploring the side streets without meeting other men in uniform.

Invariably, one had to report at Étaples (Eat-Apples in Tommy language) where one encountered the main military base just outside Boulogne. It was a bleak place among the sand dunes, tufts of grass and sea winds. The nearby resort of Paris Plage offered some distraction. Almost everyone has heard of the sandy, tented training ground known as the 'Bull Ring' where the instructors were famous for their ferocity. Not surprisingly, there was a mutiny at Étaples later in the year—although the army tried to hush it up. When a battalion had a vacancy for an officer, they simply sent in a request to the base depot at Boulogne and newly arrived officers reporting often had no idea where they would be sent. Once settled in his new abode in Belgium, Alex wrote of his personal journey along this well-beaten path:

At last the day has arrived to leave for France and rejoin the battalion. Unfortunately I am not feeling too fit after the chill influenza whatever it was, and have now developed a violent pain over my left eye which comes on after breakfast and disappears generally after lunch. At Waterloo I met Parr [Captain V. H. Parr] who has got his orders simultaneously with mine. We travel together.

I had an altercation with a porter who debated whether looking after my luggage might interfere with his lunch.

'If you take on a job you must see it through' I said.

This appeared to him to be an unnecessary severity. In any case, he saw fit to leave my luggage on the platform although he did not scruple to receive my shilling.

I was caused endless trouble at Southampton and much expense recovering the lost luggage. I was determined not to leave for France without it, and eventually caught the boat with only ten minutes to spare.

Our wanderings in France lasted a week. We landed at Le Havre and spent Xmas night with the 36th IBD, eating our plum pudding and turkey among strangers. Next day we left for Rouen. I, [was] OC train with 100 Canadian officers in my charge. They were all colonels and majors and very helpless. I was looked upon as a glorified station master or guard, expected to find seats and generally nurse the party.

Rouen was reached without accident in the morning. The weather was fine, and the break in the journey was not unpleasant but for the eye trouble. A visit was paid to Rouen Cathedral and much enjoyed. The fine architecture, stained windows and ancient tombs carried us back through history to the beginnings of England under the Romans with whom Rouen is closely associated. The tomb that had enclosed Richard Coeur de Lion's heart, stone engraved John Duke of Bedford and many others were familiar records of long ago study of English history.

At 5.00 p.m., on another train, housed in a second-class carriage, with no heating and a broken window we continued our journey to Etaples. Due to arrive about 4.00 a.m., we slept stretched on the narrow seat and awoke at 7.00 a.m. to find the train stopped in a cutting, hard frost on the ground and a dull sky overhead.

Enquiries elicited the information that there had been a collision ahead. A Belgian Red Cross train had been run into and there were several casualties among the already wounded. We were halted all day and did not complete our journey until 1.00 a.m. next morning when we were turned out neck, crop and baggage in the pouring rain and left to find our way to the rest camp where there was the possibility of obtaining shelter for the remainder of the night, while our kits lay in the soaking rain. We obtained a promise from an MP that a tarpaulin would be spread over the kits and trudged off.

Our first thought, with little knowledge of Etaples was an hotel, and to an hotel we went. Knocking loudly at an hotel door in the early hours of the morning had a savour of last century travelling. The wet, cloaked travellers, the inhospitable, shuttered house, a loud and violent knocking on the portal—the atmosphere was correct, and yes, a window hastily opened above our heads.

'Who is there?'

An uneven contest of words in French ensued, with everything in favour of the window, flow of language, barred door everything. The window won and came down with a bang.

Back through the dark and mud to an unknown rest camp we went, dreaming of bed, who had so lately been dissatisfied with the warmth and comfort of a London hotel. Across a windy hill to huddled huts on a mess plain, knocking at doors where a light showed, shaking the shoulders of sleeping men in squalid quarters, we came at last to a QM stores where was light and warmth and tea. A party from the train who had not gone hotel-hunting had paved the way for our comfort, and soon we were discussing the change of circumstances and our wanderings. A couple of blankets were spread for each on the floor and we slept.

Next morning, after a crowded shave and wash, no putting on of clothes to waste our time and keep us shivering we were able by the light to take stock of our surroundings. The mess was soon found and we breakfasted. Two days were spent there and we got our final orders for our final railway trip on Saturday night. Eye very bad.

On New Year's Eve we were once more underway before it got light. A stop of half an hour at Calais giving us a chance for tea in a cosy corner run by voluntary lady workers for men and officers. Long oval rolls split and spread with potted meat, large handsome buns, light flakey pastry vanished in the assault. It was our midday meal after a 6.00 a.m. breakfast. Bridge was played in the train but my eye prevented my joining.

At 5.30 p.m., Bailleul was reached. A long stop at Hazebrouck delayed us. But to be met by a 7th Inniskilling on the platform, luggage seized, horses waiting and a note from H.F [Harry]. It was indeed a coming home again. No other battalion was met, and the other officers travelling with us, after surrounding me as though I was their mother, vanished towards some officers club. The note was to say that there was a battalion dinner at Kemmel Chateau at 7.30 p.m. and we were expected. Kemmel Château indeed! The property of Hennessy ***!

We rode away in the dark through unknown country, through Locre where we halted for a while at the club and found the 7th Inniskillings in force. Captain S, QMR and HFR and subalterns. [Probably Captain Stainforth or Captain Seaward, Quartermaster Reid, Henry Francis Reid.] Hazell, now of the Flying Corps was there, an old 7th Inniskilling man, he was bidden to the dinner. Another two miles on from Locre in the dark we rode and now came the boom of cannon, the old familiar. We were fitting in again to our place in the long line.

A night ride on a strange road for that matter creates something of a delicious stir in one's being, known perhaps in few other forms of action. The cool breath of night, perhaps a gentle spotting on one's face of a shower, the light ribbon between dark hedges stretching away God knows where, dark drifting clouds over a rim of moon, and above all, beneath one, the horse, the warm willing faithful horse, ears a-cock, lips tatting at the bit, and sure feet planted to a rise and fall that sends a steady glow through one's arms and body, to a flame in one's breast and brain. Such is my memory of the sensations: you must excuse the poverty of my pencil.

But what of the ride with the distant burst of cannon and the flicker and flash of unpeaceful lights in your eyes? Ah, then one is indeed engaged on a great adventure, and the unknown lies ahead.

We came to the moated grange in the darkness, and handed over our horses to an orderly. We crossed the footbridge which might have been a drawbridge. Large squelching rats vanished from our feet like shadows as we stumbled around the brick causeway. A big door was thrown open in a blaze of light; and wraps removed, there burst on our gaze a long table glittering with glass and cutlery, laden with the good cheer of the season. The genie of the lamp had been at work.

Alex's arrival at the château was heralded by frothy, irrepressible hilarity and loud guffawing. After a few drams, everyone warmed to the occasion and it turned out to be an unforgettable Hogmanay—celebrated as it should be with cherished friends, some family and a stranger or two. The inappropriateness of this lavishness so close to the frozen trenches where men were shivering with cold and fear would not have occurred to many officers. It is recorded that the general made a point of visiting every unit in the division over this period, but no mention is made of him actually visiting the trenches.

At Christmas time it had been the turn of the 7th Battalion to be in the trenches, and although there was some grumbling at first, the more philosophical among them realized that it was not an everyday occurrence. The enemy was not in the mood to fight over the festive season but some shells were sent over on Christmas night to provoke him. No response was forthcoming. Christmas day was peaceful but the slaughter began on St Stephen's day with renewed spite and some men of the 8th Battalion were hit while playing football. At the convent in Locre, Father Doyle said Mass at midnight for a congregation of five hundred officers, men and a sprinkling of nuns. A young soldier, with the trace of a Dublin accent, gave an enchanting rendition of *Adeste fideles*—the Latin version of 'Come all ye faithful'.

Once back at Kemmel Shelters, the men had been given a belated Christmas meal. The menu was put together with typical Tommy humour: 'petit poisson de tin cans' and 'les petit pois vert de tin cans'. Pudding was served 'avec sauce blanc mysterieous'. In reality, the above-named 'treats' were not much of an improvement on the usual Maconochie (tinned meat and veg) or bully beef. Except for in the most adverse circumstances, one could count on a hot meal—typically stew supplemented with thick biscuit, plum or apple jam and slabs of cheese. Some said it was better

1 Officers of the 3rd Battalion (militia) Gordon Highlanders—William Thomas Reid standing back row right. (*Tom Reid Collection*)

Above left: 2 Margaret Reid in later life. (*Tom Reid Collection*)

Above right: 3 Alexander Daniel Reid as a Gentleman Cadet at Sandhurst. (*Tom Reid Collection*)

4 A troop of Imperial Light Horse cantering along the beach in the direction of Swakopmund. (*South African Department of Defence Documentation Centre*)

5 Conquering army of shaggy Boers and soldiers in tattered khaki paraded proudly in the main square of Windhoek. (*Ditsong National Museum of Military History*)

6 Imperial Light Horse followed by infantry on the march. (*Ditsong National Museum of Military History*)

7 Officers of the 7th Battalion Royal Inniskilling Fusiliers in Ireland in June 1915.
(*The Museum of the Inniskillings at Enniskillen Castle*)

Standing from left to right: Lt A. C. Taggart; Lt D. H. Morton; Lt T. Olphert; 2nd
Lieutenant H. B. O. Mitchell; Lt E. Gallagher; Lt J. Ritty; 2nd Lt M. J. Daly; 2nd Lt W.
J. Flood; 2nd Lt G. L. Henderson; 2nd Lt A. E. C. Trimble; Lt R. N. Murray; 2nd Lt T.
F. Hazell.
Sitting from left to Right: Capt. V. H. Parr; Capt. R. G. Kerr; Capt. W. D. Chambers;
Maj. A. D. Reid; Maj. R. L. Blosse; Lt-Colonel M. Hughes; Major M. G. Kenney; Lt A.
L. E. Brownlow; Capt. W. R. Roe; Lt Braddell (2nd Bn).

Above left: 8 Lieutenant H. F Reid – Battalion Transport officer. (*Tom Reid Collection*)

Above right: 9 Major A. D. Reid – Battalion Second in Command. (*Tom Reid Collection*)

10 This champion rat catcher had no allegiance to either side. Note the Lewis gun in a cover. (*South African Department of Defence Documentation Centre*)

11 The paper war was unrelenting no matter what the conditions. (*South African Department of Defence Documentation Centre*)

12 Even while in the trenches, the men could count on getting a hot stew. (*South African Department of Defence Documentation Centre*)

13 A 'bay' is a recess cut into the side of a trench for sleeping, cooking and for toilets. (*South African Department of Defence Documentation Centre*)

14 A deep dug-out offered reasonable protection against all but the heaviest shells but the trenches themselves would be wrecked and offered no protection against a direct hit. (*South African Department of Defence Documentation Centre*)

15 First picture in a sequence showing a raiding party gathering themselves prior to going through wire. (*South African Department of Defence Documentation Centre*)

16 Second picture in the sequence showing an officer leading the raiding party out on its deadly mission. (*South African Department of Defence Documentation Centre*)

17 At the Somme, before Guillemont, it was raining as it always did during a major offensive. (*South African Department of Defence Documentation Centre*)

18 Artillery moving up past a mine crater on the Somme battlefield. (*Ditsong National Museum of Military History*)

Above left: 19 The sketches of war artist, Muirhead Bone, typically portrayed picturesque pastoral scenes, detached from actuality, but this is good representation of the battalion headquarters near Kemmel which Reid described—complete with network of trenches and stovepipe jutting through the wall. (*James Bourhill Collection*)

Above right: 20 Headquarters in the front system, dug outs covered by corrugated iron 'elephants'. (*South African Department of Defence Documentation Centre*)

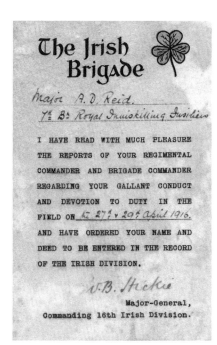

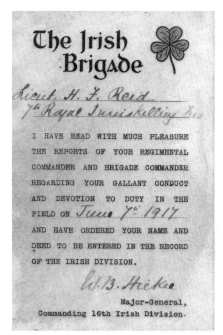

Above left: 21 Irish Brigade Parchment Certificate awarded to Major A. D. Reid for his actions during the gas attack at Hulluch. (*Ian Reid Collection*)

Above right: 22 Irish Brigade Parchment Certificate awarded to Lieutenant H. F. Reid for his actions on 7 June at Wytschaete Ridge. (*Ian Reid Collection*)

Above left: 23 Major A. D. Reid's Mention in Despatches for his cool control of the battalion at Leuze Wood. Note the signature of Winston Churchill. (*Ian Reid Collection*)

Above right: 24 The DSO had traditionally been given for distinguished service anywhere, but post 1916 it was restricted to officers who had behaved gallantly while in contact with the enemy. (*Ian Reid Collection*)

25 The result of a heavy strafe on German trenches. (*South African Department of Defence Documentation Centre*)

26 A British battalion passing through a village in Flanders on their way to the rear for a rest. (*Ditsong National Museum of Military History*)

Above left: 27 Menu for a celebratory dinner hosted by officers of the 7th Royal Inniskilling Fusiliers following the successful attack at Wytschaete. (*James Bourhill Collection*)

Above right: 28 Vickers machine gun, specially allocated for the purpose, aimed at low-flying aircraft crossing the front line near Ypres. (*South African Department of Defence Documentation Centre*)

29 A wide swath of countryside west of Ypres was covered with the detritus of war while a constant flow of new supplies was brought up. (*Ditsong National Museum of Military History*)

30 A 'corduroy' road in the vicinity of Glencorse Wood. (*Ditsong National Museum of Military History*)

31 Forward of Glencorse Wood was a place called Dead Mule Gulley—for obvious reasons. Only the stench cannot be portrayed. (*Ditsong National Museum of Military History*)

32 Both men and mules were liable to be swallowed up by the mud of Flanders. (*South African Department of Defence Documentation Centre*)

33 Attacking troops gather in a support trench awaiting orders to go forward—East of Ypres. (*South African Department of Defence Documentation Centre*)

34 German prisoners carrying their wounded through the ruins of Ypres. (*Ditsong National Museum of Military History*)

35 Infantry returning from the front system over the snow-covered ground. (*South African Department of Defence Documentation Centre*)

36 Artillery follows behind the infantry on an icy road where blackened tree stumps and debris are reminders of past battles. (*South African Department of Defence Documentation Centre*)

37 The results of an all too common strafe on the road—note the cemetery on the right. (*South African Department of Defence Documentation Centre*)

38 French civilians making their way to safety. Two British staff cars overtaking. (*South African Department of Defence Documentation Centre*)

HE whom this scroll commemorates
was numbered among those who,
at the call of King and Country, left all
that was dear to them, endured hardness,
faced danger, and finally passed out of
the sight of men by the path of duty
and self-sacrifice, giving up their own
lives that others might live in freedom.
Let those who come after see to it
that his name be not forgotten.

*Lieut. Col. Alexander Daniel Reid, D.S.O.
Royal Inniskilling Fusiliers*

Above left: 39 Harry Reid in the Cariboo district of British Colombia. (*James Bourhill Collection*)

Above right: 40 Harry Reid and his young wife, Eustasie, on a visit to the United Kingdom in the 1950s. (*James Bourhill Collection*)

Left: 41 Almost a million such certificates were sent to the families of British soldiers who died in the Great War. (*Ian Reid Collection*)

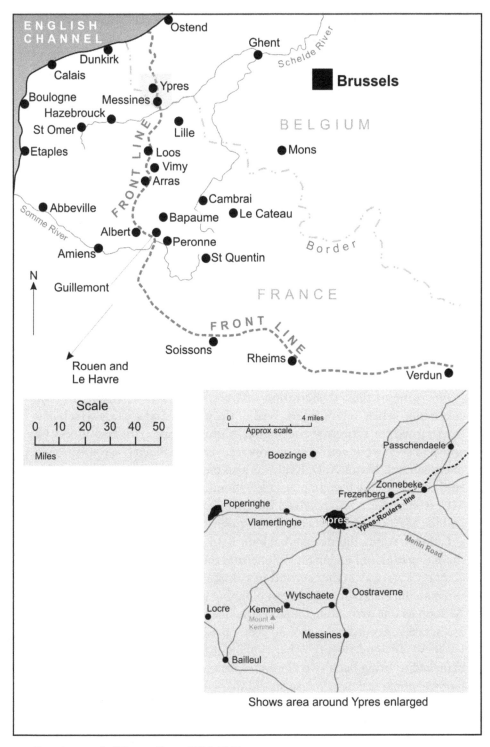

Overview on the Western Front 1916–1917.

than they got at home. Indeed, a farm worker from Kerry was asked how he liked army life. 'It's the finest life in the whole wide world,' he said. 'It's mate, drink, lodgin' and washin' all in one.'

New Year's Day was spent relaxing while listening to ragtime tunes such as 'Everybody's doing it' and 'At the foxtrot ball'. A recording from 'The Bing Boys' review would be played over and over, causing the gramophone to need constant winding:

> *If you were the only girl in the world*
> *and I were the only boy*
> *Nothing else would matter in the world today*
> *We could go on loving in the same old way.*

Invariably some clown would spoil the moment by singing along raucously and substituting his own made-up lyrics:

> *If you were the only Bosche in the trench*
> *And I had the only bomb*
> *Nothing else would matter in the world that day*
> *I would blow you up into eternity.*

For some of the 7th Battalion officers, there was further cause for celebration when news was received of the medals and awards which had been earned for actions at the Somme. Colonel Young, the battalion CO, who had been wounded and was now recovering in Blighty, was mentioned in despatches. Major A. D. Reid was also mentioned in despatches for his cool control of the battalion at Leuze Wood. Victor Parr was awarded the MC, Robert Kerr MC received the Irish Brigade Parchment Certificate, and the Military Medal was awarded to seven other ranks.

Colonel Young did not get back until 15 January, and Alex was given the acting rank of Lieutenant Colonel and took command of the battalion. Captain Parr was acting second in command and did not have long to orientate himself before he began planning a raid on the enemy trenches. As soon as one arrived in a new sector, one was expected that to gain fire ascendancy. Accordingly, at 7.30 p.m. on 12 January, Second-Lieutenant H. N. Woods and twenty other ranks got into the enemy trenches and managed to bring back two German specimens without any casualties. A flurry of congratulatory messages did the rounds. Woods was awarded the Military Cross and Private M. Sweeny the Military Medal. Surprisingly, for someone so willing to take risks, Sweeny survived the war.

Colonel Young's return to France coincided with the first anniversary of leaving Borden, and the CO took the opportunity of praising his men for having nobly upheld the honour and glory of their parent regiment and boasted that 'no serious crime or even suspicion of it' has tarnished their name. Prophetically, he added that the reputation such as was enjoyed would be hard to live up to in the hard times to come.

One was constantly reminded of the paramount importance of attaining offensive ascendency—accomplished mainly by patrolling into no man's land where there was a good chance of bumping into a Bosche strong post. At a time when the battalion was holding the line in the Spanbroekmolen sector in Belgium, Colonel Young insisted that each man who went on patrol in no man's land, submit a written report explaining what he had done during the night. One unhappy humourist wrote in his report: 'I was sent out last night with two other men and an NCO as a listening patrol. It rained all night and I got soaked to the skin in a shell hole. I saw nothing and I heard nothing!'

Priding itself in its aggression and élan, the 'Fighting Seventh' continued harassing the enemy throughout the winter months. The usual routine prevailed whereby the six day intervals of safety and security at Locre, in the shelter of Mount Kemmel, were punctuated by periods of discomfort and danger in the trenches. It has been said that this was one of the worst winters in European memory, but it did not match the misery of the previous winter at Loos. These were now experienced campaigners who knew how to make themselves comfortable in extreme conditions.

With the thick blood of the Scottish Highlanders their veins, the Reids had a genetic advantage in cold weather. Before Alex's and Harry's grandfather, the original Alexander Daniel Reid, migrated south to Banffshire, their ancestors thrived for generations in the Arctic climate of the Orkney Islands. Whisky was their elixir, especially that of Dufftown origin. That one had to drink it out of an aluminium mug made no difference to its rare quality.

The men's main concern was the rum ration and the mail. In the line, HQ was relatively comfortable and safe whereas the men in the trenches were exposed to both shellfire and cold. Harry's transport lines were in Locre but supplies had to be brought forward to feed the big machine. It was a time of relative peace and it was one of the rare occasions where Alex kept his diary more or less up to date. He mentioned the raid of the 12th instant—for which the 8th Battalion received the punishment, and wrote another of his very short stories:

17/1/17

The day of relief. After six days in Locre, it is time to move back into the trenches for our six days there. The weather has taken a change for the worse since our last tour in. The ground is white with snow, a white, wet, slushy snow which probably will not last. The wind blows warmer and we will likely have rain which will make conditions under foot worse than ever.

After a small raid on the 12th, the 8th Battalion suffered on the night from an intense bombardment on their front line. I understand it has been blotted out, and the RE [Royal Engineers] are putting in most of their time repairing. The casualties were one killed and eight wounded—comparatively light.

We rode up as far as Kemmel. The horses were very fresh in the snow. Dawn did a succession of pig bucks down the road; she as a rule, so white, looked exceedingly dirty against the virgin snow.

19/1/17

The battalion headquarters here may be described as comfortable and on the whole compares favourably with our quarters in billets whether at Locre or Kemmel. In the first place, they are compact and one does not have to travel long distances from mess to orderly room. In the next place, there is a real first rate brick fire place such as one gets in the living rooms of houses in British Colombia. This fireplace was built by the RE [Royal Engineers] after designs of the 7th Inniskillings. It is the pride of the brigade.

Although the mess is comfortable, it is not much to look at. A very much ruined farm house has been rebuilt and added to with material at the disposal of the troops in the field. Sandbags, corrugated iron and baby and other elephants are in evidence. The latter are iron semi-circles with deep corrugations which will support a heavy weight of protective material to resist shell fire. The result is an untidy agglomeration of buildings not unlike one's idea of a prehistoric village. Smoke issues from odd corners of walls and doors or jagged holes, to the distress of loiterers. But loiterers are few.

The mess room is a stone-flagged room lined with burlap. A long table fills the centre. At one end is the door and brick fireplace aforesaid. The only light comes through the upper panel of the door. An electric bell communicates with the kitchen which is accommodated in a cellar. The cellar floor is in a chronic state of flood, a hole has been dug in the lowest level from which the water is ejected through a narrow grating by means of a pump. The food is carried up a broken inconvenient staircase and passed through a hole in the wall to the mess room. A crude sliding shutter covers this hole when not in use.

My bedroom is a small room, 8 x 12, roofed by a large elephant and protected by sandbags. At the end you enter, is the door and one window. On the left is a bed of wire netting stretched on boards. On the right, various home-made articles contribute the furnishings, a table, a dressing table and a chair. An oil drum converted into a stove with a stovepipe through the wall supplies the heat. The floor is boarded.

What was once garden and orchard, but now is a waste of tangled vegetation surrounds the little tower. Trenches more confusing than any puzzle, zigzag in every direction, surround the place as an island and eventually lead by circuitous route towards the firing line some 1500 yards away.

Imagine the family party sitting down to dinner 8.00 p.m. All is uncannily quiet, since the snow fell, scarcely a shot has been exchanged. Suddenly, a clamour outside. A knock comes at the door.

'Come in. What is it?'

'Please Sor, the pushing party has arrived for the rum'.

While in the trenches, a tot of rum is served out to each man. The pushing party is a party that pushes the trucks.

'Yes, it's late today.'

'Hang Sergeant Joyce, what can he be doing.'

'Here he comes' as his head is seen bobbing above the trench of approach. An accident has happened to Sergeant Joyce. He fell in a shell hole, the papers have got wet.

'Never mind the papers. Any letters?'

'One for you Sir.'

'A miserable looking thing. Only one?'

There is generally one lucky individual who collects the bag for the day. The others have their turn next. Half an hour is devoted to the papers in front of the fire and then back to the office to deal with correspondence or a trip round the lines to visit the companies fills the afternoon.

THE HOLY OF HOLIES (A VERY SHORT STORY)

All was peaceful in the dingy orderly room. There was no presage of any danger. The industrious scratching of pens, a stifled cough and the stertorous breathing of Corporal McStick-in-the-mud were the only sounds that disturbed the silence of the soporific atmosphere. 'I'm due to get these returns finished for the CO before tea', said the corporal in his slow way, as he continued methodically to fill in sheet after sheet.

The CO had gone out and the inner room, the sanctum, the holy of holies, was for the moment empty. Had anyone been watching the partition door, he would have seen a thin spiral of bluey vapour curling through the crack of the door ajar, expanding, rising and mingling with the air of the clerk's room. As time went on, the spiral increased in volume permeating the room, until the atmosphere became so dense that one could not see one's hand in front of one's face. Still the staff wrote on.

Suddenly Sergeant Woodbine feeling the smart in his eyes, and the increased discomfort of breathing, woke up.

'My God' he said, 'gas!' and felt for the gas respirator which was not there.

All sprang up and where was peace, was pandemonium.

'Sound the alarm!'

'Where's my helmet?'

'I'm done, I'm done. Someone has pinched my respirator.'

'That's mine. Yours is under the table.'

All at length adjusted their gas masks except Corporal McStick, who with a thoughtful frown stepped towards the COs room and pushed open the door. A volume of smoke enshrouded him and drove him back coughing.

'I thought so' he said moodily. 'That new-fangled stove of the colonel's is smoking.'

Then he put on his goggles and without another word went back to his table to finish his task in the thick, but otherwise harmless fog.

The End

Divisional headquarters was at Locre where the battalion was housed in a hutment camp on the outskirts of the village on the road to Bailleul. The officers and various company messes were distributed throughout the village and there was a convent where the kindly nuns made a fuss of the Catholic boys. The men much preferred Locre to Camp Kemmel or Kemmel shelters which was on the safe side of Mount Kemmel about two miles west of the village on the Kemmel–Locre road. Kemmel Château, which was north east of Kemmel village, very close to the line, is now the site of a Commonwealth cemetery but there are other Châteaux in Kemmel which did survive the war. Battalion HQ was called 'Fort Victoria'. No sooner had the men settled into one place when they were sent to another. For a spell, on 3 March 1917, the battalion was moved to Curragh Camp in the direction of Westoutre. A wide swath of countryside behind the lines was given over to military use—camps, headquarters, stores, training and recreational facilities.

At Poperinghe, the beer brewing vats were used as baths while in the Locre district, the men could look forward to a good delousing at the baths in an old sugar-beet factory. Officers frequented the *Frontier Café*, flirting relentlessly with Mademoiselle and Maman who served cut sandwiches and *vin blanc* at one Franc per bottle. Tennis parties and dances were arranged with the nurses from the surrounding casualty clearing stations.

Inevitably, the men were kept busy with organized sport and other entertainment. In barns and school buildings close to the front, concerts were put on by professional entertainers to raise morale. Entertainments included cinema shows—Charlie Chaplin was a universal favourite. Variety shows were organized by the men themselves in the base camps. The most talented in the regiment would perform time and time again. Gilbert and Sullivan type acts were put on by ensembles calling themselves 'Quartette True Till Death', 'The Horrible Four' and 'The Crumps'—which was the term of endearment for a German 150 mm shell.

On one occasion, while the 7th Inniskillings were on the march, a smoking concert was held—without a piano. Private Knight was the star of the show with his rendition of a song called 'The clothes horse'. The refrain being that the only horse which he would care to ride on was the one the missus dried the clothes on. By the time the battalion had left the Somme, many of its best performers were gone. At Locre, where 'smokers' were organized by the YMCA, the individual talent was provided, as usual, by Sergeant Joyce and Private Phillips who performed the popular choruses 'A little bit of heaven', 'Absent' and 'Michigan'. On occasion, the men of the battalion were loaded onto lorries and taken to concerts put on by the adjoining 36th (Ulster) Division.

Brothels flourished in the larger centres like Dunquerque—a fact which was normally kept from those at home. However, their existence was sufficiently acknowledged by the army for there to be separate facilities for officers and other ranks. For those who preferred something more refined, *sans* the certainty of venereal disease, the 'resort' of choice was Bailleul, just over the border in France but close enough for a day off. 'Sports' days were held with monotonous regularity. Events included a bomb throwing competition, tug-of-war and other schoolboy favourites such as the three-legged race and sack race, pick-a-back race.

Mules and horses played a leading role in many a competition. While at Noeux-les-Mines on 27 July 1916, a brigade horse show had been held within shelling range. Incongruous though it may have seemed, the horses were well turned out, sleek with their summer coats, every buckle of their harness gleaming. Predictably, in the officer's charger event, Colonel H. N. Young won first prize and Major A. D. Reid came second among all four battalions of the brigade. Perhaps to humour a close friend, G. A. C. Walker recorded for posterity in the battalion history that it was due to the 'care and efficiency of Lieutenant H. F. Reid that the battalion transport won most of the important events' such as field kitchens, wagon driving and pack mules. The transport officer, for his sins, was also expected to give riding lessons to officers who couldn't ride.

On another occasion, an 'assault-at-arms' was held which involved bomb throwing, retreat beating and platoon drill. Some new exhilarating events which the army introduced to the world of competitive sport involved the putting up screw-pickets and barbed wire. When left to their own devices, the men played football. A game of 'footer' would take place under any conditions—even under fire.

Saint Patrick's Day was a holiday for the whole battalion and every Irish battalion HQ received a consignment of shamrock—a tradition dating from the Boer War or before. Green ribbon was lavishly displayed as the companies marched to their chaplains to celebrate mass. Brigade sports took place in the afternoon but on this day, the events were mostly of a comical nature—like the wheelbarrow race. There was great amusement when the officers ran a cross-country course and a few fell out from complete exhaustion. In the inter-company cross-country run, the first one home was that man—Private M. Sweeny MM.

That evening, a list was published in routine orders of the twenty men who had been awarded the Irish Brigade Parchment Certificates for gallant conduct in the field during 1916. Once again Sweeny's name was among them. The highlight of the day was a variety show known as a Pierrot show. The Pierrot troupe was organized by Captains Seaward and Robinson who called themselves the 'Green and Buffs'. At this time, Captains Parr and Kerr were still commanding 'A' and 'B' Companies while 'D' Company was under the command of Captain Stainforth. Truly, theirs was a unified family—officers, men, horses and, even if only in spirit, friends recently departed. Alex, the adjutant, and 2IC of the battalion, was the paterfamilias. The singing of 'Take me home to dear old Blighty' brought everyone close to tears and the rendition of Alex's own personalized composition raised the barn roof:

17/3/17 (St Patrick's Day)
Do you ken the commander of Company 'A'
He's a rare man to talk at any time of day
If you can get him on his legs he'll have something to say
From nine to three a.m. in the morning.
Chorus

Yes, I ken Captain Parr and Shiny Tip too
Kerr and Seaward and all the crew
I ken them well and so would you
If you met them very early in the morning.

Do ye ken the commander of Company 'B'
He's up from England on a weekend spree
We like to have him, his girth to see
For he tends to embonpoint: it's a warning.

Chorus as above

Do ye ken the commander of Company 'C'
Who drills the subs and the trainer he
Of the Green and Buffs—they're the cure for me
When I'm feeling a bit groggy in the morning.

Chorus

Do ye ken the commander of Company 'D'
A portent sum potentate when issue is free
He has minus ten men, but he drills plus three
With the hounds of hell in the morning.

Chorus

Do ye ken the CO and orderly room staff
When they put on their gaspirators you may laugh
From a snort to a roar, from a roar to a strafe
From a strafe to a FPI in the morning.

Chorus

Yes I know the orderly room in the morning grey
It's my habit to go in there day by day
Subscriptions, buttons, badges I have got to pay
Oh, but I'm broke, yes I'm broke in the morning.
Do ye ken the quartermaster who never feels blue
Jackets, Service, Dress, he will issue to you
And government watches, not a few
God knows where they have got to by the morning.
The transport officer so they say
Built his own lines but the RE had to pay
Now he's going to have to move far away
How absurd! Don't you think so in the morning.

Chorus

Ay, I ken the quartermaster and transport too
They live in Locre, sound, from their point of view
And will ask you down to dinner, play bridge till two
And pay well for your pleasure till morning.
Do you ken the ally man with his draughts and pills
He'll cure your fevers and prevent your chills
And if you are suffering from any real ills
Will think about a Blighty in the morning.
And you ken the second in command, ah me
A long, lean, lank-like looking thing is he
And he wants to know, and he wants to see
Who the, where the, what the, why the in the morning.

Final chorus

Yes I ken all the fellows of the 7th 'Skins'
With their bright brass badges, spit and polish wins
And the Bosche will answer to them all for his sins
At a very early hour one morning.

CHAPTER 9

Wytschaete—the Ecstasy before the Agony

Without doubt, the pinnacle of the Fighting Seventh's participation in the war to end all wars was the Battle of Wytschaete—more commonly known as the Battle of Messines. Much has been written about this battle which is best known for the exploding of nineteen massive mines under the German trenches prior to the attack. Messines lies at the southern-most part of the Ypres sector, and was one of the strongest points in the German line.

The overall objective was to take and hold the long ridge running north—south from Hill 60 near Ypres through Wytschaete to Messines two-and-a-half miles further south. In effect, this would be a prelude to the Third Battle of Ypres, the objective of which was Passchendaele Ridge. The 16th (Irish) Division was to be in the centre with the 19th Division on their left and the 36th (Ulster) Division, which also had service battalions of the Inniskillings, was on the right. To a large extent therefore, this was an Irish show.

From the north end of the ridge, the enemy could observe troop movements over a wide area. The only way to dislodge them was to mine under their trenches and explode tons of dynamite. The tunnelling was going on under the noses of everyone during their stay in the Locre—Kemmel area, two miles west of the deadly ridge. Secrecy was of course paramount, and the blue clay which came out from underground had to be got rid of surreptitiously. Tunnellers were paid six shillings per day as opposed to the usual one shilling for it was dangerous and unpleasant work requiring special qualities.

Some weeks before the big day, the division was sent to the quiet countryside further to the rear where they could train without being watched by the enemy. On 13 April, the battalion left Locre and spent the next few days on the march towards St Omer. *En route* they passed through the main square in Bailleul onto the Cassel road—one of the main supply routes in northern France, and spent the night in shabby billets in the big transit centre of Hazebrouck. The following day's march which took them through Ebblinghem, Renescure and Arques to Wizernes was about sixteen miles and particularly arduous because of the heat combined with the weight of the equipment. Billets *en route* varied from the quite comfortable to the unspeakable.

On the third and final day of the march, the country was more hilly and the stones harder. That evening, in the rain, they passed through St Martin-au-Laërt, Moulle and Nordausques—all forgettable names in forgettable places. Yet, a modern-day pilgrim in these parts will find the towns and farms little changed. In the years immediately after the war, an industry sprang up around the battlefields to cater for family members retracing the last steps of their dead husbands, sons and fathers. But even then, few will have visited these agricultural villages where multitudes of men rested their worn-out bodies and stressed-out minds. The cult of the fallen soldier was centred on the monuments and cemeteries.

The final destination of the brigade was a relatively attractive village called Zouafques surrounded by green fields where the many platoons of the brigade spread themselves out in different hamlets and assorted farm houses. Easter was celebrated in this northern part of the Pas-de-Calais. If the padres are to be believed, the faith and fervour of the Irish lads made an impression in the village.

The training ground was about two miles outside Zouafques, and by 1.00 p.m. the men were back in the village for the midday meal. Afternoons were given over to sports—all of which would be played wearing some assortment army uniform. Inter-battalion and inter-brigade matches were organized and at first attracted much interest but then became boring. A fair proportion of the time was spent on the rifle range near Moulle. During one exercise, the men were required to advance in extended formation firing from the hip. Much ammunition was wasted on another occasion when the officers tried their hand at firing the Lewis guns and got carried away.

The climax of this training period was the 49th Brigade's great rehearsal attack carried out on a replica of the trenches at Wytschaete. No amount of detail was spared, even the creeping barrage was replicated by a line of flag-waggers and side-drummers. All went well apart from a chewing-out from the brigadier for not wearing steel helmets. In fact, the area was seething with red tabs among which were counted Major-General Sir W. B. Hickie, Lieutenant-General Hamilton Gordon, Corps commander, and General Sir Herbert Plumer, the 2nd Army commander who had been entrusted with the whole operation.

Every officer was summoned to attend the post-exercise conference where General Plumer expressed his wish that the officers should explain to their men, the objects for which they were fighting—and that was ostensibly to free Belgium. He went on to express the opinion, that this was the beginning of the end. By contrast, when the padre explained to the men the reasons why they were in this struggle, he spoke in a simple, homely language which they liked. He reminded them that they were defending their homes and families and friends in Ireland.

On 27 April, the anniversary of the gas attach at Hulloch, the General (GOC) sent a most complimentary letter to Lieutenant-Colonel Young congratulating the battalion for upholding the noble traditions of the Royal Inniskilling Fusiliers and expressing the hope that they would do so again in the future. To the sceptical rank and file, it was just more ominous-sounding claptrap.

The next morning brought the start of a three-day, fifty-mile march back along the same route to Carnarvon Camp about two miles north of Locre. Without any pause for rest, the brigade took its place in the line in the Diependaal sector. The trenches there were little more than breastworks because of the high water table. On 9 May, the sector came in for an intense bombardment during which 'D' Company headquarters was blown to pieces, Captain D. Hollis, only just returned from leave, was killed by a direct hit from a '150 mm'. He and the three other men killed were buried in the new battalion cemetery at La Laiterie—so-named after a dairy farm, situated between Ypres and Kemmel. The remainder went back to Birr Barracks, Locre to make final preparations for the offensive.

When the battalion arrived back in the Locre area, their strength was counted at 30 officers, 670 other ranks and 55 horses. Another 60 other ranks joined soon after. For the coming battle, Alex was to stay behind in the 'B' Echelon. Experience of high casualty rates had led to the practice of leaving approximately 100 men of all ranks from each battalion out of battle to form a nucleus in the event of heavy casualties. Certain battalions had been reduced to 200 men after such an offensive as this. As the brigade transport officer, Harry was involved from start to finish and his personal account of the battle begins at the preparation stage:

For the operation, I was put in charge of transport for the whole brigade. Two or three weeks before the battle, I was called to a conference at the divisional headquarters on the question of pack animals and their equipment for carrying ammunition to the front line during an engagement in place of the regulation army limber GS (general service) wagons which were useless owing to the heavy shelling prior to an engagement which destroyed the roads. Pack animals were to be substituted. These were mainly mules which could be led over or round the worst places. All officers were required to attend the conference.

The Quartermaster General, several staff officers and my brigadier were present. My sergeant and NCOs had devised a type of light carrier to fit securely on the pack saddle of the mule, which could be easily loaded and unloaded.

I produced a mule at the conference, saddled with the carrier fitted to the saddle. There ensued a discussion among the staff officers on the desirability of using this equipment. Not one of them was familiar with the conditions under which transport operated and had no practical knowledge of the matter. Junior officers dared not open their mouths but after listening to the discussion for some time, I ventured to say that the equipment had already proved itself under the conditions for which it was intended and in my opinion, it could be relied on.

As I spoke, I saw the brigadier's complexion take on a reddish glow. He evidently considered that I had spoken out of turn, or should not have spoken at all. The QMG however said with a laugh of genuine amusement, 'Well this officer is the man on the spot and carries out the work. He ought to know'. The brigadier relaxed and the meeting ended.

Fatigues were particularly onerous during the fortnight building up to the offensive. Birr Barracks was a hive of activity. Big guns were arriving every day and ammunition heaps and aerodromes sprang up all over the countryside from St Eloi to Armentières. Even in the rear area, dug-outs had to be strengthened to prepare for the artillery duel which would inevitably ensue. Assembly areas were identified and communications trenches dug. Alex was responsible for ensuring that each platoon and company knew what its objectives were and to ensure successful liaison between them. The failure of one section of the line could have disastrous consequences along the whole front. At Scherpenberg Hill near Locre, a huge three-dimensional scale model of the battlefield could be viewed from a raised cat-walk surrounding it. Officers spent many hours studying the model together with maps, aerial photographs and intelligence reports.

Preparatory fire reached new levels of intensity, and 2,000 artillery pieces pounded the enemy defences for many days. Of course, the enemy reacted with equal measure and the transport camp was not spared. Although accustomed to seeing the suffering of horses, the images of one nightmarish incident would remain with Harry forever:

One night in particular, our camp was heavily shelled. We were in an open field and there was no cover. We had to scatter the horses, each man leading a pair. The shapes of men and horses were indistinct in the darkness. One could see here and there horses which had been hit, swaying on their legs, endeavouring to remain upright, their entrails hanging down, trailing on the ground.

Regardless of the distress which the transport people may have experienced, Brigade would not entertain any excuses in the event that they could not perform their duty on the day. Horses were highly valued. Transport men had to be good horse-thieves as they often made up their shortages with stock from other battalions who were not keeping a watchful eye.

In the final hours before zero-hour, a conference was held at battalion headquarters and all company commanders were summonsed at once. The commanders of 'A', 'B' and 'C' companies arrived at the 'Holy of Holies' in good time and after saluting the CO, took their places. Captain Stainforth was late and an orderly was sent to call him. After a few minutes, the orderly returned with the message that Stainforth was dressing and would be along shortly. Another orderly was sent with the instruction to tell him to come as he was. Stainforth came running with one side of his face shaved, the other covered with lather and a shaving brush bobbing in his hand. This scene lent a bizarre and humorous touch to what was otherwise a serious business. Incidentally, the meeting lasted an hour and a half, by which time the soap had crystallized on the man's skin.

One last going-over of the operation orders: Communication trenches allocated to the 49th Infantry Brigade to be Watling Street (in trench) and The Fosse (out trench). In addition to the cross-country routes, the roads in the forward area allocated to the 16th Division were the Kemmel– Wytschaete Road (Suicide Road) and VC Road. Equipment to be carried was clearly specified. All officers were to be dressed and equipped the same as the men; sticks were not to be carried. Haversacks were to be worn on the back, except for Lewis gunners, rifle bombers and carrying parties who were to wear it at the side. Each man to carry 120 rounds of small arms ammunition and two Mills bombs—one in each top pocket.

The 16th (Irish) Division had decided to attack with the 47th Brigade on the right and the 49th Brigade on the left with the 48th Brigade in reserve. The 7th Royal Inniskilling Fusiliers and the 7/8th Royal Irish Fusiliers were detailed to take the red and blue lines, the 2nd Royal Irish Regiment were ordered to move forward to take the green and black lines. The 8th Royal Inniskilling Fusiliers were to act as 'moppers up' to the brigade. The names Grand Bois, Petit Bois, Spanbroekmolen, Oostraverne Wood and Wystschaete village were committed to memory forever.

Each officer's responsibilities were spelled out. Unit commanders were to send reports to Battalion HQ every half hour; all commanders down to platoon commanders should keep in touch with the commanders of similar formations on their flanks; deep dug-outs in enemy lines were on no account to be entered, except with permission from an officer—mainly because of the threat of booby traps; all ranks except stretcher bearers were strictly forbidden to stop and assist the wounded; the order to 'retire' was to be absolutely ignored. Watches were synchronized three times daily under the supervision of the signals officer.

On the night of 6/7 June, the assault troops moved to the assembly areas in silence. Strictly no lights were to be showing. Bayonets, helmets and buttons were dulled with mud—which was fortunate because at about 1.00 a.m., an enemy aircraft flew over looking for any signs of activity. As per instructions, the men stood dead still and did not turn their faces upwards. Mass was said at 1.00 a.m. Then at 2.30 a.m. the two chaplains put on their battle kit and made for their respective aid posts.

The suspense of waiting was the worst. Father Doyle was one of the 80,000 men who stood ready to go over the top. His nerves were 'jumping about like so many mad cats'. Friends shook hands, few could eat but all swallowed the thick rum, about half a wine glass was given to each man. Those less hardened to battle and liquor found it difficult to keep down.

At 3.10 a.m., the battle commenced with the detonation of the enormous mines which had been burrowed under the enemy lines during the preceding months. A total of twenty mines had been laid along the entire front. Only one failed to explode. From Kemmel, one could hear a deep muffled roar. The explosion could be heard in southern England. Columns of smoke, flame and earth shot up hundreds of feet into the air, the whole area swayed as if it was an earthquake, the trenches felt like they would collapse. The ground went up and came down again—like a huge mushroom and the men began cheering as though at a football match.

As the tons of clay and rock fell back to earth, dust obscured everything and hindered the advance. Some men were forced to wear their gas respirators just to breathe. Shells screeched overhead and the earth was going up in front due to the creeping barrage. It was found that the enemy line had been completely blotted out and within twenty minutes, the Irish had taken their first objective. Casualties were light and had been mostly inflicted from being too close to the creeping barrage. Father Doyle, the Catholic padre, was always at the forefront and witnessed the charge of the Irish Brigade:

> Before the debris of the mines had begun to fall to earth, the 'wild Irish' were over the top of the trenches and on the enemy, though it seemed certain they must be killed to a man by the falling avalanche of clay. Even a stolid English Colonel standing near was moved to enthusiasm: 'My God!' he said, 'what soldiers! They fear neither man nor devil!' Why

should they? They had made their peace with God... they were going out now to face death, as only Irish Catholic lads can do, confident of victory and cheered by the thought that the reward of heaven was theirs. Nothing could stop such a rush, and so fast was the advance that the leading files actually ran into the barrage of our own guns, and had to retire.

As the Irish advanced over the shell-torn no man's land, the artillery bombardment intensified. The enemy was completely demoralized but the German gunners recovered to do some firing of their own. The overriding impression was one of sweltering heat and devouring thirst which comes from the excitement of battle. Some told of physical weakness from lack of food and soreness of feet. Tanks now came up and rendered useful help although they were hardly needed. A number got 'ditched' and had to be towed out.

The attack penetrated as far as the 3rd German line, passing by some terrible sights. Prisoners were running towards the British lines, having no need for an escort. The advance was not to be held up for the work of collecting prisoners so the order was given to let them through. Some who did not surrender fast enough were shot. German officers who tried to arrest this flight were liable to be shot by their own men. In a short time, the wounded began to come in, a number of wounded Germans among them. A wood (previously called 'Unnamed Wood' was captured by the 'Skins' and given the name 'Inniskilling Wood'.

At 6.50 a.m., the Royal Irish Regiment passed through the blue line and proceeded to take the final objectives, the green and the black lines and the furthest objective was taken by 3.10 p.m. It was an impressive sight to see the artillery galloping up and coming into action in no man's land. The guns were able to cross the front system on bridges which had been previously erected and fired down from the eastern slopes onto the enemy's new positions.

Casualties were mercifully light in relation to the objectives gained and the magnitude of the operation. The dead and wounded amounted to 146 officers and men. Of these, twenty ORs (other ranks) were killed or died of wounds. Within three hours of the attack, the crest was secured and the 7th Battalion was ordered back to their starting line—which could now be considered a rear area. Sightseers took a great interest inspecting the huge craters but were not allowed down into the crater because of the poisonous fumes of the explosives. Within two days, the 7th Battalion was back at Wicklow Lines in Locre.

The capture of the Messines—Wytschaete Ridge was one of the most successful operations of the war and messages of congratulation flooded in from all quarters, including the Commander-in-Chief, Field Marshal

Douglas Haig and the Corps Commander who said, 'Well done! 16th Division. Heartiest congratulations on the capture of the black line. I fully realize what a magnificent effort by each individual this has been.'

The transport lines of the four battalions were situated half way between Locre and Kemmel. Each battalion had its own transport under one officer, and for this operation, Harry was appointed Brigade Transport Officer in charge of combined transport. His part in the battle on 7 June was to bring up water, ammunition and rations and to distribute them among the forward troops. Water was brought up in petrol tins and the tepid tea was carried up in tins insulated with straw. Throughout the night Harry was engaged in transporting ammunition to the men of other units who were holding the new front line. Proudly, he told of his own role in the historic battle:

The new front lines were now about one-and-a-half miles beyond Wytschaete village towards the village of Oostraverne where the enemy had entrenched themselves and were preparing for a counter-attack. Supplies needed to get up to the troops as soon as possible. The operation had to take place at night as a line of 50 pack animals and men in single file winding over the ridge in daylight would attract enemy observation with unpleasant consequences. The ammunition had already been dumped by the Army Service Corps at a point in the support line. I had a map which traced the route to our destination in Oostraverne. The brigade pack-train moved off from the transport lines at twilight and reached the loading point in the support line before it got dark. By the time we were loaded and ready to leave, darkness had fallen.

Ahead of us was the sombre, shell-torn ridge and the continuous thunder of our own and the enemy's gun fire. A muddy path was all that remained of the road shown on the map, all other features had been destroyed. The path took us around the southern side of Wytschaete village, down the slope towards Oostraverne and through the forward line of our massed field guns which were aligned wheel to wheel along the length of the ridge. The guns were firing continuously and gave an exhilarating expression of power and victory. Our fire for the present appeared to have subdued the enemy who were bringing up their reserves.

We arrived at our destination and the men unloaded the ammunition and supplies as quickly as possible so that we could get back and bring up a second load. Provided that we moved in the dark, we had no reason to fear direct fire from the German guns. On the other hand, if we were sighted, we would have a poor chance of getting back. Time was critical and the only way we could make it up was by loading quickly since the pack animals could not go faster than walking pace.

My watch told me that without mishap, we had time to reach the forward dump and return to our side of the ridge before daybreak. I was making my calculations with some anxiety when the sergeant came forward and informed me that the men refused to make another journey. The party of men was made up of an equal number from the four battalions from the brigade—only a quarter belonged to my battalion. Generally, Irish soldiers are loyal to their own officers. The Southern Irish as soldiers, or in any other occupation, are not particularly amenable to discipline and the transport men were not so firmly and frequently drilled as the men of the companies. The work required of them does not require the same level of control. Also, I was dealing with temporary servicemen, not regulars.

The sergeant who had come to inform me of this was a fine type of regular army NCO of many years' service in a famous Irish regiment. He had seen active service in India and elsewhere in the Empire. I told him it was imperative that the second journey was commenced without delay as otherwise discovery by the Germans in the daylight would result in failure and our own destruction. 'I understand that Sor', he replied. I told him to line up the men and I would speak to them. In as few words as possible, without commenting on the danger involved, I emphasized the importance of the work required of them. They were dismissed and soon I was informed by the sergeant that they had rapidly recommenced loading the animals. The sergeant added, 'What you said was exactly right Sor'. Coming from a regular and experienced NCO to a temporary soldier, I took this as an acceptable compliment, particularly as it concerned men from the south of Ireland. As some anonymous officer once said: 'An Irishman is difficult to drive but easy to lead.'

A fair margin of time had been used up but at least we were on the move again and commenced our ascent of the ridge. When we reached the summit, dawn was breaking. A flat stretch of country lay beneath us. The guns on both sides were firing without cessation and bursts of shrapnel filled the sky. The enemy was now retaliating with vigor from their new positions. As I feared, we reached the forward dump in daylight. As the men were unloading in anxious haste, an officer came to me from a concealed position close by and said, 'My commanding officer wishes to know how long you are remaining here and requests that you go at once before you draw the enemy fire'. I replied that I fully understood the position and would leave immediately the ammunition was unloaded. While we were speaking, a ranging shell fell exploded 100 yards short of us. The officer signed for the ammunition and returned to his entrenched position. The animals were getting restless and another shell exploded in a direct line towards us. This time about fifty yards short.

The off-loading was now completed, the men started to file out and when the last man and animal had gone, the sergeant and I turned to follow. Almost immediately, the final ranging shell exploded behind us where we had just been standing. We were away just in time, the column spread out at intervals in single file ascending the ridge. The enemy's fire did not follow. We were no longer a stationary target, without cover, to be annihilated.

Some months later, I was informed on good authority that my brigade had made a mistake and should not have issued instructions for the supplies to be sent forward, which was the reason I did not receive the Military Cross for which I was recommended.

Although Harry did not get the MC he so badly wanted, he was commended for his actions early on in the day, bringing up and distributing water to the troops. It had been a sweltering day and water was badly needed on the battlefield. He was one of twenty men awarded the Irish Brigade Parchment Certificate for gallantry and devotion to duty on 7 June 1917.

A wave of optimism followed the Battle of Messines Ridge, and no doubt at home in their cushy clubs, old men devoured the newspapers eagerly. Feeling elated, the battalion arrived in Merris once more for a rest in the exquisite French countryside between Bailleul and Hazebrouck. After one day there, for reasons unknown to the rank and file, they were ordered to march back to Locre and then, on the 16 June, marched straight back to Merris again. The men were thus occupied on the day that one of their own was executed. Private John James (Jimmy) Wishard was the only member of the 7th Royal Inniskilling Fusiliers to be shot at dawn, though it was by no means uncommon—especially in Irish regiments.

Wishard had gone missing in Hazebrouck on 31 March, then headed for Boulogne where he remained on the run for three weeks before being arrested. A military policeman spotted him and asked him to give an account of himself—which he could not do. Two days later, he was back in Hazebrouck but managed to escape from the billets and once again made for Boulogne. This time he stole a revolver from Lance-Corporal Hughes who had been sleeping next to him. Eleven days passed before he was picked up at the docks, in civilian clothing, trying to board a ship.

After a preliminary investigation, Major A. D. Reid approved the charge sheet and the court martial took place on 29 May, which also happened to be the first birthday of the unfortunate man's daughter. A friendly witness, known as a 'prisoner's friend', Lance-Corporal C. N. Walker, testified that Wishard had always been of good character and had done well in the trenches. He pled not guilty, stating that the only reason why he had deserted was to get home to see his wife and child. The last time he had received word from them had been in December, saying that his baby daughter was sick. He had applied for leave to go home to County Omagh but was refused.

The court martial consisting of three officers, two of whom were from the miscreant's own battalion, found him guilty on two counts of desertion and sentenced him to death as military law dictated. The final decision to carry out the sentence would have rested with General William Hickie or even with General Douglas Haig himself. Unlike some other officers, Hickie was all for giving a man the chance to redeem himself. In most cases, the death sentence would be mitigated but Wishard's life was not spared.

As was customary, the priest spent the night with the doomed man, preparing him for his fate. Shortly before dawn, he was led out and tied blindfolded to a post. The medical officer pinned a white marker over his heart so as to direct the aim of the firing squad. One of the rifles contained a blank round thereby permitting each individual to believe that it may not have been them who was ultimately responsible. At 3.58 a.m. on 15 June 1917, the sentence was carried out. Death was instantaneous and the body was buried in the yard of the gloomy, Gothic-looking church in the centre of Merris. His grave has since been moved. Wishard, sometimes mistakenly written Wishart, was one of 306 British soldiers who were executed for various crimes—mainly desertion or cowardice in the face of the enemy.

Little thought was given to the shame that was brought on the family, with the accompanying economic hardship since the next-of-kin of executed soldiers were denied the usual allowances. Alex cared about his men, but the battalion came first and he would have wanted to prevent any further lapses in discipline. The good record of the battalion may have been upheld but from now on there was a perceptible change in the relations between officers and men.

The very next day, as if nothing had happened, the senior officers sat down to a feast in celebration of their great victory at Wytschaete. The brigade commander, General Leverson-Gower, was present and during his visit, amid another round of back-slapping, he commented: 'You must remember that these big fights are historic, and this action will be held up to your sons as a battle well worth studying, and your sons will say, my father was there'. Alex kept his original copy of the menu for the celebration dinner in the back of his note book. It was a most memorable occasion.

The last two weeks of June were spent moving about the French countryside, far behind the front line. It was the first decent rest which the battalion had enjoyed in two years. Much of the time was spent at Merris but on 20 June they began moving north. A few days were spent at Eecke before moving on to Buysscheure Farm near Saint Omer—only twenty miles inland from the Channel port of Calais. This untroubled landscape was soon covered by canvas, and despite the blazing heat, sport was a daily obligation. The men were allowed to go into St Omer and wander around the streets, visiting little *estaminets* and cafés. The more devout or cultured among them visited the cathedral. Leave was generously allowed at this time and on 25 June Alex allowed himself ten fleeting days of special leave. This would be the last time he touched British soil.

When he arrived back at Battalion HQ which was now at Tatinghem, just outside St Omer, on 5 July 1917, Alex was given news that was both gratifying and devastating at the same time. The good was that he was being promoted to Lieutenant-Colonel and the bad was that he was being attached out to another battalion in a different division altogether. In *The Sprig*, Oxo Young wrote a farewell tribute to 'one of its [the battalion's] oldest and truest supporters'. Alex had served with the Seventh for almost three years. 'It was due to him, and he alone, that the magnificent spirit of *esprit-de-corps* and bond of true brotherhood existed between all ranks.'

It was therefore not happenstance that Alex was chosen to lead the 1st Royal Irish Rifles, which was part of the 8th Division. The entire division was in tatters and the 1st Royal Irish Rifles had the worst disciplinary record in the division—despite the many death sentences which had been imposed. Alex Reid was considered the best man to galvanize this band of misfits in preparation for the coming offensive in the Ypres Salient. At the age of 35, on 7 July 1917, Lieutenant-Colonel A. D. Reid officially became the OC of the 1st Royal Irish Rifles.

CHAPTER 10

Westhoek Ridge—
Frezenberg Ridge

Approaching Ypres, one immediately felt the tension in the air. This sector was well known to be extremely hazardous to one's health. The salient had been relatively quiet for a while but since the Messines Ridge show there was the expectation of another big offensive. Previously, there had been two struggles of attrition at Ypres. The second battle, infamous for the trial use of gas, was fought over these same fields during the spring of 1915. The Canadians had borne the brunt of it that time and it seemed that the ground was still impregnated with the poisonous fumes.

The 8th Division (of which the 1st Royal Irish Rifles was part) was thrown into the epi-centre of the Salient which comprised the wedge between the Menin Road and the Ypres–Roulers railway line. Their task was to attack directly in front of Ypres in the direction of Bellewaarde Ridge rising slightly from Hooge which is about two miles out of Ypres on the Menin Road. The Germans, as usual, held the high ground and had a perfect field of fire—looking down into the basin.

Behind the lines, tens of thousands of men lived in tented camps and temporary billets. The build-up of materials attracted shelling by long range guns. Observation balloons wallowed in the sky, easy prey for enemy aircraft intent on creating havoc. Officers had been taught that it was useless to follow an aircraft with machine gun fire, it was better to saturate the sky with fire from numerous guns and let the aircraft fly into it. For this purpose, and for defence in the event of an infantry attack, divisional machine guns were sited in an irregular line about 1,500 yards behind the front line. In front of this line, there could be isolated guns in concealed positions, able to bring flanking fire on important points. 'The machine gun is for the defence of an area, not a locality'—this according to the notes in Alex's correspondence book under the heading 'A lecture in Locre'.

On the edge of the Ypres inferno was the thriving town of Poperinghe whose delights were legendry. On occasion, it was subjected to long range shelling but most of the civilians remained. A good living could be extracted from the hundreds of thousands of troops who passed through here. Prior to the war, 'Pop' had had nothing to recommend it, but now the shops sold books, post cards, fountain pens and gramophones. A faded poster for Sunlight Zeep still clung to the wall of the post office. Here and there one could feast one's eyes on a pretty girl.

'Pop' was not exactly the 'bright lights' but it offered some creature comforts. Talbot House, called Toc H in gunners signalling code, was an institution where rank was not observed, which was convenient for those who had brothers or friends in the ranks. Situated in a three storey building with creaking wooden floors and a chapel, one could get a good meal, relax and write letters. Around the piano, to the tune of *Sous les ponts de Paris* they sang:

> *Après la guerre fini*
> *Soldat Anglais parti*
> *Mademoiselle in the family way,*
> *Après la guerre fini*

Out of his familiar circle, where friendship had cancelled out all sorrows, Alex met up with the 1st Royal Irish Rifles at Dominion Camp, in a wooded area between Ouderdom and Vlamertinghe on 8 July 1917. That unlucky battalion had just returned from a particularly traumatic tour in the front line during which the battalion HQ had received a direct hit from a heavy shell. The surviving officers knew that they would soon be making a big attack from the trenches which they had been holding.

The very next day, this mixed bag of officers and men entrained at Ouderdom bound for a training area around Tournehem just across the French border near Zouafques where the 7th Inniskillings had spent happy days in the spring. Now, the new CO of the 1st Royal Irish Rifles set about knocking his battalion into shape. Alex had the gift of being both friend and commander and Captain Whitfield, the second in command, wrote of this period 'The colonel rather frightened us all and sacked some of the HQ staff right away. I liked him very much. He was very thorough indeed.' Daily lectures were part of the intensive preparations. From scale models and aerial photographs, the officers studied the ground and then drew up a thorough plan of attack.

Because of the high water table, the Germans had built a system of concrete blockhouses. Some of these were multi-chambered, holding about 40 men, raised a yard or two above the ground, with a low entrance at the back and bristling with machine guns. The British did not take the trouble to construct such permanent fortifications as pill-boxes. They were deemed not worth the expense and considered to be detrimental to the offensive spirit. In fact, the smaller pill-boxes were easy to make. A wooden or corrugated iron frame was bought up in the night and filled with concrete. They were impervious to all but the heaviest guns and even then, difficult to hit. The barbed wire defences were cleverly designed to channel the attackers into their killing zones. All but the biggest shells would bounce off these concrete bunkers but some got completely turned over, tossed up in the air—foundations and all.

In training for their impossible task, a certain Colonel Wylie presented a lecture on the employment of machine guns in attack and defence. While some might have taken the opportunity to catch up on sleep, Alex contentiously made meticulous notes in his brown book, which verify that concrete emplacements were not favoured by the specialists. His notes will be of interest to those concerned with the imperatives of the battlefield:

> The [machine gun] emplacements should be concealed by natural means in unlikely places and not built up with much work so as not to draw fire:
>
> Concrete emplacements for guns with covered tops and loopholes for fire are not considered suitable. There should be a deep dug-out in which the team can take cover in a heavy bombardment and from which they will emerge on its cessation, but while in action they will take their chance with the others. Men prefer to see all round them to be able to bring fire to bear on any quarter in an emergency, rather than be cooped up in a small chamber, choked by the fumes of the guns discharge, unable to see more than a small section of country in their immediate front through a loophole.
>
> Machine guns should not be used to gain ground but can be used to hold ground already captured. They will therefore support the advancing troops from their defensive positions until the troops have made their objective and emplacements have been prepared for them, when they will be brought up to assist in holding the ground gained, and join in the next forward move.
>
> When an attack is proposed, the action of the machine guns must be carefully considered. From the maps issued, a careful study must be made of the German trenches and wire at a distance of 1,500 yards behind their front lines. Obvious positions of their machine guns will be surmised. A close study of the ground behind in the neighbourhood of one's sector may be invaluable when the day comes to advance.

For two weeks in warm weather the battalion trained together and played together, cultivating an *esprit-de-corps* of sorts. The battalion history relates that the men were in good spirits, however, it might be more accurate to describe their mental state as one of having a deep sense of foreboding mixed with a tinge of anticipation. A week before Armageddon, on 24 July, the men marched to Audricq were they were loaded into open railway trucks and taken back to the Salient. The primary detraining station before Ypres was a place called Hopoutre, surrounded by bleak hop-gardens, and re-designated 'Hop-out' by the troops who had their own pronunciations for all foreign-sounding place names.

On 16 July, the British bombardment commenced and the Germans responded in kind. Heavy shells began tearing up hitherto untouched land. The tranquillity of Vlamertinghe Château was broken by the thunder from great guns which squatted in fields of poppies between the trees. While camped in readiness near Poperinghe, Harry observed the constant flow of traffic up to the front and listened to the incessant roar of the preparatory bombardment as those in the first wave prepared to go up to the start line.

Slabs of beautiful Beech wood had been used to construct roads and bridges up as far as the Ypres-Yser canal so as to bring the guns and supplies up closer to the front. This was done at night and then camouflaged. Grenades, mortar bombs, and duckboards had been carried to depots and dumps close to the front line. New 'corduroy' roads and great heaps of war materials began to appear and the shadow of death was sensed by all.

From time to time, Alex would be asked by fellow officers and men to put his signature to a hastily-scrawled one-page will. Since death was a general expectation, there was nothing remarkable about a man making out his last will and testament. Newly arrived subalterns were especially advised to make sure their affairs were in order. Second Lieutenant Robert Kelly Pollin, a twenty-year-old trainee solicitor from Belfast, made out his will four days before he died. Another doomed subaltern of the 1st Royal Irish Rifles was Second Lieutenant Hugh Brown, also from Belfast, who had transferred from the 5th Hampshire Regiment after the death of his brother in that regiment.

The 7th Royal Inniskilling Fusiliers were in reserve at the start of the Third Battle of Ypres, but the battalion moved up to the front system on 6 August, and were to be involved in the second phase. The only eye witness known to have documented Alex's final hours was Captain G. Whitfield, the adjutant of the 1st Royal Irish Rifles. In any case, the view of events as experienced by those who lived them was limited to a few yards of heaving mud, obscured by smoke. A good overall view can be found in the narrative of the 8th Division's operations on 31 July which was compiled within a week of the battle, but it appears to have been primarily an attempt by the general staff to justify themselves.

The approach march from Pioneer Camp to assembly positions at Halfway House began at 10.00 p.m. on 30 July. All companies having reported present, they proceeded on their way, going by a cross-country route. Alex and Captain Whitfield led the way—their nostrils assaulted by the stench of dead horses on top of the sickly smell of asphyxiating gas. Blinding flashes pierced the blackness all around them as the great counter-battery bombardment opened. Flares continuously rose up from the German lines in a visible display of nerves.

Floundering along in the dark in single file, carrying heavy weights along duckboards, progress was extremely slow. With gas helmets further obscuring their vision, men were falling over debris and into shell-holes. Those in front mumbled 'mind the hole' to warn those behind. Soon after crossing the canal a message came back to say that the Germans were shelling Shrapnel Corner. This was one of the busiest and most unpleasant places in the Ypres Salient, beyond which point, it was said, a man should abandon all hope. It was on the main route and situated about a quarter of a mile from Ypres on the Messines road. Luckily, owing to a lull, the whole battalion got past with only one casualty.

Halfway House, a strong point about a mile behind the front, was reached at 3.50 a.m.—just as the first wave was going off. It had previously been arranged that all men should be under cover but this was unfeasible, the men just flopped down and fell asleep, seemingly oblivious of gas and high explosive shells that came over at frequent intervals. Alex, together with his two senior officers, then went through the low, slanted entrance into the bunker, which was half under putrid water in which there lurked all manner of offensive matter. This was a substantial bunker and overflowing with humanity but a small recess had been reserved for Alex and his entourage. It was a miserable shelter for what was to be his last night on earth. All three sat on a bed and in five minutes were asleep, but only for one very short hour.

It was an oppressive night and dawn seemed unable to penetrate the overcast sky. The first wave went into the attack at 3.50 a.m., and on reaching the German front line, found that the trenches had ceased to exist—blown to kingdom come by the barrage. Some Huns were still alive and came scrambling out of bunkers with their hands up. Tossing in a few bombs as they went by, the line of men struggled to keep up with the creeping barrage because of the condition of the ground. Hostile aircraft swooped low overhead and directed a barrage of accurate fire. A few hundred yards further on, they ran into deadly machine gun fire from

German concrete blockhouses, particularly from two points named Kit and Kat, north of Westhoek. The first wave consolidated and a counter attack was driven off accounting for around forty of the enemy but they could not entirely reach their objective—the aptly named black line.

Now it was the turn of the second wave and the 25th Infantry Brigade which consisted of the 1st Royal Irish Rifles in the centre, the 2nd Lincolnshires on the right, and the 2nd Rifle Brigade on the left. Their intention was to pass through the black line and proceed to the ultimate objective—the green line running west of Zonnebeke village through the western edge of Polygon Wood—so named because it was once bounded by roads on four sides.

At 6.30 a.m., it was erroneously reported that the first phase had been successful and across a wide area, the three battalions went forward confidently. According to the war diary, the battalion advanced in artillery formation whereby the unit is dispersed into a diamond formation with sections spread out. It is the balance between control and vulnerability often used in the approach march. With Alex at the head, the battalion converged on the German front line (already taken by 23rd and 24th brigades). Little shellfire was met with and all arrived safely by 8.30 a.m.

When the barrage for the attack on the green line was commenced at about 9.30 a.m., the battalion followed their colonel forward again. The battalion war diary states that they advanced 'with spirit and in perfect order', but in reality they stumbled along with shoulders hunched as if against a driving wind and rain. A withering fire tore through the ranks as they passed through the blue line which was held by the leading brigades. Clearly, friendly troops were not altogether in possession of the black line on Westhoek Ridge as the commanders believed.

Enfilade machine gun fire from the direction of Kit and Kat held up the company on the left. The company on the right got pinned down just short of Jargon Trench by interlocking fields of fire from Glencorse Wood and Nonne Boschen. They tried making short rushes but the casualties just piled up. In spite of many heroic efforts, the right company could go no further and proceeded to consolidate. Dutifully, Alex started off up the slight incline in the direction of Glencorse Wood to see what the hold-up was. He did not get far. Anyone watching would have seen his body jerk as the bullets ripped into him, then crumple.

Without their colonel, the centre company got as far as Hanebeke stream, which was now a bog. A determined few even got across the stream and made some progress up the western slope to within a short distance of the green line but they could not maintain their isolated position. At about noon, these brave souls began to withdraw to Jabber Trench on the reverse slope of Westhoek Ridge, where the rest of the battalion had ground to a halt.

At this critical point of the battle, reserve companies were brought up and all resources committed. Twenty tanks were allotted to the division and were a complete failure. Several were hit, the rest bogged down. Tank commanders were criticized for their inability to appraise the military situation but the crews did give support with their dismounted Lewis guns. A graveyard of tanks could be seen at a place called Clapham Junction— just beyond Hooge, off the Menin Road.

A miserable grey vapour crept over at about 1.00 p.m. and by 4.00 p.m. the rain was pelting down. The sponge-like earth quickly became waterlogged. This lowland had once lain under the sea—it was reclaimed marshland, and as is generally known, the constant shelling had destroyed the natural and man-made drainage.

The enemy employed their favourite tactic of 'elastic defence' whereby the wings hold firm while the centre gives way temporarily before a counter attack. But the mud hampered them almost as much as it did the British. The rain was an impartial opponent. The enemy rushed up fresh troops to Zonnebeke by lorry and were punished by British artillery. When the counter-attack came, it reached the trench held by the centre company of the Royal Irish Rifles who hung on tenaciously. On their exposed right, the Linconshires were driven right back to their own front line.

The few remaining officers rallied their men and launched a vigorous counter-attack. In turn, the Germans were driven back, leaving behind many dead, and the Irishmen gave up no ground. General Clifford Coffin, CO of the 25th Infantry Brigade, in a rare exploit for a man of his rank, walked about from shell hole to shell hole encouraging the men in continuous fire. He seemed to lead a charmed life and at one point brought up ammunition himself. He was one of at least twelve who won the Victoria Cross on that day, and as well-deserved as they may have been, countless acts of equal valour went unrecognized.

Darkness came early, and the brigade withdrew leaving in their wake a harvest of dead and wounded. Corpses lay thickest on Westhoek Ridge within sight of Glencorse Wood beyond. The divisions standing by to relieve the 8th Division gave up their attempts. It should be remembered that this fiasco was being replicated along a much wider front. As a result of the day's operations, the division had gained 2,000 yards but Westhoek Rridge was still in enemy hands.

That night was miserable with a cold driving wind, drizzling rain and a quagmire underfoot. Ambulances filled with the wounded and dying made their way through the ruin and desolation of the city of Ypres to the rear. Ammunition wagons and extra guns made their way to the front. Heavy guns continued roaring throughout the night.

At 10.30 p.m., Captain Whitfield who was now in command, tried to get the message through to his scattered battalion that they had been relieved and should retire to the old German front line. Few received the message but in the early hours of the morning, in the dark, stumbling through shell holes lip to lip, some of the surviving Irishmen staggered back to their starting point at Halfway House. The intention was to withdraw to the blue line behind Bellewaarde Ridge where their HQ was situated. Out of the twenty officers, six were killed, (five of them subalterns) and out of the 620 other ranks, thirty were killed, 145 wounded and eighteen missing.

The Brigade HQ remained at Bellewaarde which is where Harry pitched up the next day in search of his brother's body. Bellewaarde Lake is at Hooge, on the left hand side of the Menin Road. In wiser days, the lake had been surrounded by ornamental trees and paddocks all overlooked by a château with steep gabled roofs and wrought iron balconies. Now the only structures were the pill boxes which changed hands more than once over the years.

By the end of August, parts of Glencorse Wood had changed hands eighteen times—such was the strategic value of the Westhoek Ridge to the Germans. From Westhoek, they overlooked the entire town of Ypres and could call down artillery fire on any movement. In a small localized attack on 10 August, the place known as Westhoek was finally taken— thereby pushing out a small bubble in the line. On 31 July, however, the position was still overlooked by Glencorse Wood and Nonne Boschen which remained in enemy hands. Even if Alex's body had been lying in an accessible place, it is doubtful that anyone from his adopted battalion would have taken the trouble to bring it in for burial. Like forty thousand other men at Passchendaele, Alex simply vanished as earthly clay.

Captain Whitfield kindly wrote that, 'Colonel Reid who had been in command but a short time, had already won the affection and confidence of all ranks.' In truth, there was no one in this band of strangers who would have cared much about his fate, having known him for only three weeks. Alex's former commanding officer and close friend, Colonel Oxo Young, placed a notice in the *Sprig* saying, 'His loss was deeply felt by all who knew him and had served under him'. But even these words, though sincere, did not convey the true feelings of his fellow officers with whom he had lived side-by-side, through agonies and ecstasies.

But there was no time for former comrades to grieve, for on 6 August the 7th Royal Inniskilling Fusiliers moved into the front line, passing en route the debris and shell holes from the battle of 31 July. The location of the outpost line which they held ran through Frost House to a point fifty yards south of Pommern Castle. About 150 yards to the front was Beck House, a strongly fortified concrete pillbox from where the Germans could spray fire on any movement. Battalion headquarters took occupation of

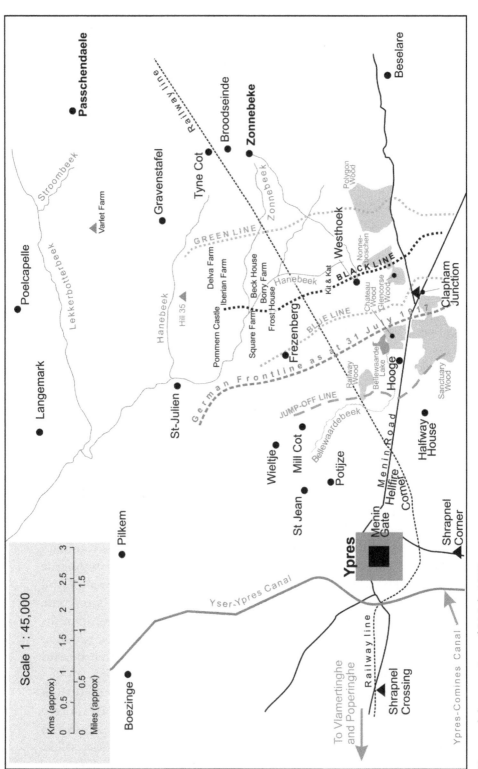

Ypres and the operations of 31 July 1917.

Square Farm which had been used by the enemy as an aid post and was relatively untouched. This position benefited from a good water source as well as a good view of the enemy positions. With five feet of reinforced concrete on top, it was also comparatively safe. As it happened, during Colonel Young's occupation, it would be put to severe testing as the enemy used it as a target for the calibration of his artillery.

The time spent here was perhaps the most uncomfortable of any time the battalion had spent on active service. From dawn to dusk, the troops forward of Square Farm were unable to move because of snipers and machine guns. During daylight hours, men simply had to sit tight in water-logged holes in the ground. On the morning of 8 August, Lieutenant T. H. Shaw and Sergeant S. Carroll were reported missing. It was assumed that they had lost their bearings in the dark and walked into the German lines by accident. Evidently, they were not taken prisoner as they were never heard of again.

The 7th Inniskillings were relieved on the night of 10/11 August and travelled by train back to Toronto Camp, near Brandhoek—midway between Vlamertinghe and Poperinghe. On no previous occasion had Harry seen a dirtier, more disheveled company of men return from the line. So caked in mud were they, hardly a rifle or Lewis gun was in working order and the ensuing three days was spent in preparing equipment for the continuation of the offensive. Harry's own preparations did not go smoothly:

The transport camp comprised the transport of the four battalions of the brigade and was under my charge. Fifty men were detailed to keep the troops supplied with ammunition during the coming battle, each battalion supplying its quota. Our camp was not immune to shelling and in one particularly heavy strafe, the quartermaster's store was wrecked. The senior quartermaster asked me to telephone Brigade to obtain some counter-fire, which I did, and was answered by one of the brigade staff at HQ which was comfortably underground at a place called Mill Cot. For some reason, my request was met with derision—a response which magnified my contempt for this species of officer. Fortuitously, his objections were overruled by the authoritative voice of a battalion commander whose line had been crossed with mine and who had heard our conversation.

A few days before the attack, I received written instructions from Brigade HQ informing me of the disposition of men and horses at zero hour. I found that I had been given a position which, while clearly shown on a map drafted some months previously, in actual fact was inaccessible. Since our arrival, I had thoroughly surveyed the terrain. In all directions, the rain-soaked ground had been churned up by shell fire and turned into a muddy swamp. To reach the position given me, with the animals laden with ammunition would be impossible. It was not unusual for brigade staff to devise plans and issue orders whilst having no practical knowledge of the existing conditions.

On this particular occasion, the brigade staff had arrived at their dugout in the support line at nightfall, red tabs glinting, and immediately descended forty feet below the surface of the ground. Not only would my party of men and horses have bogged down in a morass under enemy observation and been obliterated in a few minutes by the German guns, but of more universal concern, the fighting troops would not receive continuous supplies of ammunition during the engagement.

Had I been a regular army officer, no doubt I would have accepted the brigade orders as a final decree of my fate, but being only a temporary one, I decided that the successful execution of my task was more important than the risk of being branded a 'dud officer' for questioning an order. Thus, I handed to the brigade messenger my own note on where I thought the transport should be stationed at the start of the attack. To my surprise, the brigadier agreed to my suggestion. In hindsight, however, the operation order which was circulated before the attack looked more like a wish list than a coherent plan.

Following soon after this flurry of messages, a salvo of gas shells burst at the entrance of the brigade dug-out necessitating the immediate evacuation of the entire staff and their replacement by other officers in the brigade. The colonel of my battalion, Oxo Young, was in command of all units in the fighting zone. Although he was next in superiority to the brigadier, a battalion commander junior to him was put in overall command of operations on the brigade front. Oxo Young remained in charge of operations in the field but had to report to an officer junior to himself.

On the evening of 14 August, the under-strength battalion moved forward to its assembly point. As a result of the previous spell in the lines and an outbreak of trench fever, their strength in the line now amounted to nineteen officers and 472 other ranks. Captain Victor Parr stood in as second in command and was tasked with setting up an advanced headquarters at Delva Farm. As was the custom, about five officers, including Major Kerr, and 100 other ranks remained behind with 'B' Echelon. Major Kerr was also eventually transferred to another battalion and was killed on 11 July 1918 while attached to the 9th Royal Irish Fusiliers. He had simply been out with his new commanding officer to inspect the wire when he was killed, thereby meriting one line in the war diary of that battalion. Robert Kerr, a chubby, fun-loving 28-year-old, would be missed by his few remaining brother officers of the 7th Inniskillings and his widow in County Wicklow.

It was the wettest August in living memory. During one spell, it rained non-stop for four days and four nights. Headquarters staff tried to keep their maps and notebooks dry under waterproof sheets. It was still raining as the men moved to the start line, each step sinking ankle deep into the mud, passing Square Farm, to take up their positions on the northern bank of the Hanebeek. At 4.45 a.m. on the 16th, the battle commenced. The creeping barrage had to creep much more slowly than normal because it was a struggle to get through the frightful bog.

Advancing across a field of corpses which had lain there since the battle of two weeks previously, the 16th (Irish) Division attacked Borry Farm and Beck House. Victor Parr gave an account of how, at the point of his revolver, he forced the occupants of a number of concrete pill boxes to surrender. He could not spare any men as an escort, so he ordered the prisoners to report at Square Farm—which they did. Bridges were brought up and the advance continued through barbed wire entanglements crossing the Zonnebeke midway between Pommeren Castle and Beck House.

At 5.55 a.m., things appeared to be going well, the 7th Battalion had reached fifty yards beyond Delva Farm, and the men took cover in shell holes. Parr heard that the unit on his left had retired and sent two runners with a message, and a duplicate by carrier pigeon, to say that unless his flanks were re-established, his position was critical. Parr's signaller had been hit by rifle fire right alongside him and not a single message had yet got through. One platoon commander nearby released a pigeon with a message tied to its leg and after a few feeble flaps, it fell to the ground. Its feathers were too wet to fly and it began walking over to the German lines. A fusillade of rifle fire was aimed at it to prevent the information from falling into the hands of the enemy. Two message dogs were allotted to the division. They carried coded messages in pouches on their collars. Runners were to be used only as a last resort.

At about 8.30 a.m., a runner from 'B' Company informed Captain Parr that Lieutenant Woods had been killed and that the Germans were counter-attacking in the direction of Delva Farm and Hill 35 which was undefended. The Germans could be seen 400 yards away advancing in two lines at about five paces interval. Parr decided to retire to Iberian Strong Point, rounding up stragglers along the way. He succeeded in collecting about forty men but there were no NCOs to take charge of them and the line gave way again. Seeing a large number of his men round Beck House, Parr resolved to make a stand there. On thinking the matter over, he decided that it would be of no value and ordered his party to return to their starting line. Under heavy machine gun fire, the stragglers, which included members of other battalions, tried to make an orderly retreat, keeping the required distance, facing the enemy. It was now about 3.00 p.m. and Parr went back to Square Farm to make his report. Victor Parr, who had been wounded at Guillemont, was now once again wounded and the DSO which he subsequently received was harder earned than most. He ended the war as a prisoner in Germany with the rank of major.

On the right, the 8th Battalion was pinned down 100 yards short of Borrie Farm. It was here, at about 3.30 p.m., that Father William Doyle, together with three other officers, was killed instantly by a shell. Doyle had been doing what he always did—giving absolution and comfort to the dead and dying. Every time he returned to the regimental aid post, he was begged not to go out again, but he would not desert his boys in their agony.

Lieutenant Harry Reid was convinced that he was lacing up his boots for the last time on the morning of 16 August 1917. His task was perhaps less hazardous than that of the forward companies although ammunition wagons were a prime target. Mules floundered in the mud and men had to push wagons stuck up to their axels but Harry was more concerned about the flying pieces of jagged iron than the condition of the road:

> In the chilly light of daybreak, I brought the men and transport from their concealed position behind the Ypres ramparts, past the support line and proceeded along the Frezenberg road to about a thousand yards from the front line when we turned left and traversed ground which gave a comparatively firm foothold but rose to a higher level. We must have now come into view of the enemy who threw up a barrage of shrapnel fire to prevent our advancing. It seemed a miracle that we escaped casualties. So close were the shell bursts above us that I could see shrapnel hitting the water in the shell holes as if it was hailing.
>
> We now turned right where the ground sloped downwards towards the front line and unloaded the ammunition at the designated dump. The men and animals then returned to Ypres in the charge of a subaltern while I continued towards the concrete bunker where I found Oxo Young and other officers who had been engaged in the abortive attack. The men, what remained of them, were back at their starting point. Tempers were short and I did not stay for long.
>
> On my journey to and from the bunker, some ingenuity was required to dodge the machine gun bullets and shells. At one particularly slimy and muddy part of the return path, a salvo of 5.9 inch shells came over my head and landed in the soft earth. A slight shortening of range, I thought, and I would also become a shower of mud. Quickly changing my direction, I avoided further trouble and arrived back at Brigade HQ.
>
> Later in the afternoon, Brigade received a message that the Germans

were advancing from three directions upon our positions and that I was to take up further supplies of ammunition. However, when I got there, I found that the reports of a counter-attack were unfounded. The firing had subsided and there was little enemy activity.

The Brigade was withdrawn from the line that night, and on 17 August got back to safety near Vlamertinghe. Shortly afterwards, two special orders were handed down. The first one announced that the 'Fighting Seventh' would be amalgamating with its sister battalion to form the 7th/8th Royal Inniskilling Fusiliers. The second order, which is reproduced here, may have brought some consolation:

Officers and men of the 'Fighting' Seventh Inniskillings: The more one learns of the battle of 16 August at Ypres, when you advanced fearlessly against fierce opposition as only true Inniskillings can, and captured all your objectives, including Hill 35, Ibernia Farm, Delva Farm, right up to the Langemark—Gheluveldt Line, and hung on there until forced back by overwhelming numbers, both your flanks having long since been exposed, the more pride one should feel in belonging to such a body of men. You have nobly upheld the honour and traditions of your battalion and parent regiment, and by your courage and devotion to duty won fresh laurels for them. Our casualties were very severe. Out of 20 officers and 472 men, who went into action, only 7 officers and 114 other ranks came out with the battalion. All ranks must now endeavour to re-form and organize the battalion so that we can be ready when called upon.

From Frezenberg Ridge, between Square Farm and Low Farm, the British looked out over a valley of the dead towards the unattainable goal of Zonnebecke. Borry Farm and Beck house had to be won and lost many times over. A small local attack was made on these two strong points by the Argyll and Sutherland Highlanders and Seaforth Highlanders on 22 August. Their divisional HQ sent an order to the effect that it should be captured at all costs but there were just not enough men. It was said that Borry Farm was defended by five machine guns and sixty expert gunners.

Incidentally, it was the South Africans who, as part of the 9th (Scottish) Division, finally took Borry Farm and Beck House during the attack of 20 September. That day's battle broke the back of the German defence in the Salient. Individuals like General F. A. Maxwell VC, the officer commanding the 27th Brigade, surely played an inspirational role by leading from the front and forsaking his steel helmet for an officer's cap, replete with red staff band. He was shot by a sniper the very next day. The general was a 45-year-old ex-Indian Army man who won his VC at Sanna's Pos during the Boer War. South Africa has its own hero of that fight. Lance Corporal William Hewett won the VC for single handedly capturing a pillbox— killing most of its occupants. This time, the counter attack was repulsed, but astoundingly the same ground was lost again in the 1918 push.

A South African who was a stretcher bearer on 20 September related in his memoirs that in the vicinity of Borry Farm he came across a 'ghost' in a German pillbox. When he had regained his composure, he questioned this apparition and discovered he was Irish and had been hiding out there since his regiment's own involvement at Frezenberg Ridge more than a month before. Somehow he had survived on putrid shell-hole water and dead men's rations.

For months, it had been impossible to remove the dead because the battlefield was always under observation. In November 1917, before the final attack, it was decided to bury the dead on Frezenberg Ridge because it was too demoralizing for the fresh troops. The burial party was given rubber gloves, sandbags, and an extra ration of rum. By now, bodies were in an advanced state of decomposition. Remains were put in a sandbag and buried with a little prayer and a map reference. If no dog tags were found, names might be found on the back of a watch or in a pay book kept in the pocket of a tunic. Very often there was no means of identification and the grave was marked 'unknown British soldier'. Approximately four out of ten corpses could be identified. There were Germans among them but they were left unburied. At Tyne Cot War Cemetery, where many of the bodies from this battlefield are buried, a large proportion of the gravestones are inscribed with only a rank or a regiment, or just the words 'A British Soldier of the Great War'. The main German cemetery at Langemark contains 44,294 burials—the majority are unidentified and are buried in a mass grave or *Kameraden Grab*.

CHAPTER 11

Abroad, Avoiding Extinction

Flanders fields and Alex Reid were both left behind as the 16th (Irish) Division moved to the Bapaume—Miraumont sector, not far from the Somme battlefields. As they moved south, Harry's ten days leave became due and he left for London via Boulogne. While in England, he received a letter from Oxo Young telling him that he was leaving the battalion and regretting in consequence that he could not get him his Military Cross for his part in the Frezenberg Ridge operations. Like most officers, Harry coveted the MC. Many were prepared to risk their lives for it, but the award did become debased as the war progressed. The DSO on the other hand, had traditionally been given for distinguished service anywhere, but post 1916 it was restricted to officers who had behaved gallantly while in contact with the enemy.

Only on his return from leave did Harry learn that Oxo Young had had a run-in with the brigadier over matters which had been simmering for a long time. One of them had to go, and it was Young who was transferred out of the brigade to a battalion of the Sherwood Foresters which was fighting on the Italian front. According to Harry, 'The whole battalion, officers and men, were genuinely sorry to see him go because he truly was a good officer. Above petty intrigues and sycophancy he gave loyalty to his men and received it in return. Besides that, he was exceptionally efficient and totally fearless. It did not pay to be honest where one was faced with favouritism and injustice.'

By the time Harry arrived in London, the holiday season was almost over but resorts like Blackpool had had a record season. Holiday makers arrived at Victoria Station on their return from the coast while hospital trains bringing the wounded from Ypres were pulling into Charing Cross Station.

Air raids were now a common occurrence. People had become accustomed to them. By 1917, bombing raids by Zeppelins and planes had killed about 3,000 people in London and various coastal towns. The danger of being hit by a bomb was not inconsiderable. Not being able to retaliate somehow made it worse than being at the front where one was accustomed to the idea of being exterminated. The twin-engine bombers, with the black and white crosses clearly visible, more often than not got away unscathed.

It was alleged at this time that England was no place for an honest man. At every turn, one encountered profiteers, politicians, autocratic non-combatants, base-dwelling staff officers and other species of trench dodgers. The story of one opportunist who got his just reward appeared in newspapers around the world, during September 1917. London was buzzing with gossip about Lieutenant Douglas Malcolm, a man of good position and ample means, who admitted to the murder of one Anton Baumberg, who called himself the Count de Borch. It was said that De Borch was a man of extremely doubtful ancestry. He was possessed of a fair amount of good looks but no particular presence, in an effeminate way according to witnesses. However he was well educated and his charms were evident by his many conquests. About six feet tall but not athletic, he used his powers with women to lure them to ruin.

The Count had been carrying on an affair with Malcolm's lovely young wife, Dorothy, while he was absent at the front. Malcolm had discovered the intrigue when he returned on leave some months previously. He thrashed de Borch and pleaded with his wife to give him up but she refused. Malcolm then challenged de Borch to a duel but the challenge was not accepted.

A few months later, Malcolm again returned to England on special leave and sought the scoundrel out at his seedy Paddington lodging house—not much different from the place where Harry had stayed, over the road from the station, two years previously. Four shots were fired and Malcolm then handed himself over to the police. Council for the defence portrayed Lieutenant and Mrs Malcolm as the victims of a foreign scoundrel. The plea was self-defence. Ultimately, the all-male jury found that it was justifiable homicide, in what was a triumph for the 'unwritten law'—that of a man's right to avenge his own or his wife's honour. Outside the court, the crowd of several thousand was uncontrollably ecstatic.

Another sign of the times was that the public had developed an interest in spiritualism. Around the dinner table, people were fond of repeating supernatural tales of phantom cavalrymen, angels, strange lights and ghostly apparitions. Of course, the clergy were condemning of this wartime epidemic of the occult but could not deter those who were crying out for help.

Bereaved parents held séances in an attempt to continue participating in the lives of their lost sons. Sir Arthur Conan Doyle, author of Sherlock Holmes, who lost his son, Kingsley, as well as his brother, was believed to be able to communicate with his son. In the last years of the war, a book called *Raymond* was particularly popular. It delved into the supernatural and psychical phenomena whereby a dead soldier (Raymond Lodge) was put in touch with his family through a medium. Kipling too explored the spiritualist world.

A more obscure book called *The Adventure of Death* by Dr Robert McKenna was hailed in the press for being able to bring balm to wounded souls by showing that death is nothing to be feared. The book was intended to be a comfort to many a reader who had a loved one in the fighting line. The author informed his followers that soldiers had no actual fear of death. 'They are borne on and uplifted by feelings too indefinite to define, yet poignant enough to utterly quench all forms of fear. Even serious wounds are not felt at the time of infliction, so strong is the wave of vitality that sweeps them ever onwards. The "great beyond" is where the dear ones we have lost are found again. They are only waiting a little way off, and the journey to them will be but a brief and pleasant one someday.'

Although England was not the Utopia which he had always pined for, Harry was not over-anxious to return to the battle area, leaving behind all that was friendly and safe. It mattered not that this was a time of war, the practical and administrative issues ensuing from a death in the family remained burdensome. Conveniently, it presented the opportunity for special leave:

My mother was the executor of Alex's will, and in accordance with her wishes, Alex's DSO was given to me. It had been forwarded to E. R. Tymms Esquire, a friend of the family, and I had to go to Chelmsford in Essex to fetch it from him. While on leave, I also managed to fit in a visit to our family solicitor in Edinburgh. My mother had been granted a very small pension for the dependent of a Lieutenant Colonel and it appeared that pensions granted to mothers of officers killed in the war were based on the financial position of the deceased officer before he joined up or was recalled for active service. The authorities had received no information on this score and had therefore awarded the lowest pension.

I knew nothing about Alex's financial position, and requested a letter from our family solicitor, Alexander Campbell, stating that it was essential I should go to Canada, straighten up matters for my mother there and obtain the necessary information to enable me to apply for an increased pension. Leave of 49 days absence was being granted to officers who had been in the battle area continuously for a period of two years or more. I therefore had two strong reasons to support my application—namely, period of active service and urgent private affairs.

Immediately on my arrival in France, I applied for special leave but the paper work was delayed because on the first application sent in by Brigade, someone had written that I was 'entitled' to it. This was returned with the terse comment that 'no officer is <u>entitled</u> to leave'. As the application had to go from Brigade to Division on to Corps, Army, GHQ France and finally to the War Office in London, during its progress no doubt resting in many office files marked 'for attention', it is not surprising that its journey backwards and forwards took about four months. The army worked in mysterious ways.

Although a soldier's life was not his own, he would often feel a sense of relief at being part of the big machine again. Having felt homeless in England, Harry braced himself for another winter in France. Passchendaele had finally fallen to the Canadians in November. Although it was a futile victory, it was a tribute to British doggedness. Shortly thereafter, at the Battle of Cambrai, considerable ground had been gained with the proper use of tanks, but then it fell to the hard-pressed infantry divisions to consolidate the new positions and dig new trenches.

The capture of a section of trench called Tunnel Trench near Bullecourt on 20 November 1917 was the 16th Division's contribution to the Battle of Cambrai. The 49th Brigade was there, but the 7/8th Inniskillings were left out of the attack. The Irish captured 2,000 yards of trench and 635 prisoners. There ought to have been more prisoners but an Irishman with a bayonet is not easily stopped once his blood is up. They counted 330 German bodies in the trenches. Surprise was the key to success, there had been no preliminary bombardment, but the 3rd Division on the right failed to capture its 800 yard section of trench

Tunnel Trench was part of the Hindenburg Line, and as the name suggests, it had a tunnel running under the entire length of it, thirty to forty feet below ground. It featured electric lighting and side chambers for storage, recessed rooms fitted with bunks for sleeping. Officers were served dinner in an underground dining room from an adjoining cut-out kitchen. The ceiling was a few inches higher than a tall man walking upright. In some places, it was crowded with men of various units, and deserted in others. It was a highway which brought severe traffic congestion at peak times. Along its vast corridors, cold draughts blew strange odours. German trenches apparently emitted a different stench to those of the British.

In this sector, bodies had still not been removed and in places corpses formed part of the breastworks. Signs were stuck on the parapets saying 'Don't dig here—dead bodies' and 'Unknown British Dead—no digging'.

When a heavy shell demolished a part of the wall, exposing a corpse, it was quickly built up again with sand bags. Supposedly this was a quiet sector but shelling seldom stopped and enemy aircraft occurred regularly overhead.

Generations of South Africans have been weaned on the story of *Jock of the Bushveld* which was authored by Sir Percy Fitzpatrick, a prominent pioneer. It is not generally known, however, that his 28-year-old son, Nugent (Percy Nugent Fitzpatrick), was killed near Cambrai on 14 December 1917. Nugent had served in the ILH in South West Africa before joining the artillery. His battery had been in continuous action at Ypres for three months and he had been promoted to Major. A fortnight before he was due for leave, the motor car in which he was travelling to the railhead was hit by a stray shell. At the time, Sir Percy was resident on his farm in the Eastern Cape where Nugent had attended St Andrew's College in Grahamstown.

A lesser-known but no less remarkable South African, who also grew up in the Eastern Cape, was Colonel John (Jack) Sherwood Kelly VC, CMG, DSO. His VC was won at the Battle of Cambrai on 20 November 1917 while commanding the 1st Battalion of the Royal Inniskilling Fusiliers. He too spent some of his school days at St Andrew's in Grahamstown. Sherwood Kelly was not a regular officer, but from the age of sixteen, fought in numerous campaigns beginning with the Matabele Rebellion in 1896. In addition to the VC and DSO he was nine times mentioned in despatches and four times wounded. In 1919, he ran afoul of the military authorities for having 'remarked adversely on matters of military import'. His wife divorced him in the following year. Her letter of ultimatum, which he rejected, was published in newspapers around the world in January 1920:

We have not lived together for a long time now—not since the autumn before last. In fact, you have only spent three nights with me since we were in Cape Town in 1916, and we were married only in April of that year. I am a proud woman and I would not beg any favours from you. If you do not want me, tell me so, and I will never trouble you again. But if you find that your feelings have softened towards me, and you would like to have me once more in your life, you will have only to tell me so and I will come. You have been very unkind ever since that trip to Africa in the summer of 1916. I think the men and women who have made you out such a hero must have turned your dear head. But remember, the day may come when you will no longer be in Khaki, and the hero of yesterday will become the ordinary citizen of tomorrow, and the latter may perhaps sigh for the affection which he despises today. God keep you—your neglected but still-loving wife.

As incongruous as it might seem, the Boer leader and author of the book *Commando*, Deneys Reitz, joined the 7th Royal Irish Rifles and became part of the 16th Division at around this time. Previously he had served in German South West Africa and in East Africa. Then, at the end of January 1918, South Africa's Prime Minister, General J. C. Smuts, a great friend of Denys Reitz, made one of his visits to the front in his capacity as a member of the War Cabinet. Few would believe that this man, now a loyal servant to Britain, had during the Boer War nicknamed his band of fighters 'The English-killing Fusiliers'.

As they sat huddled around braziers in their greatcoats, the troops retained little of the martial spirit, but in his report to the War Cabinet, Smuts noted that the morale of the division was remarkably high. Perhaps he was unaware that if an Irishman is asked by an officer 'are you cold?' the reply will invariably be 'not too cold Sor' and if he is asked 'are you wet?' he will say 'not too wet Sor'. Winter made trench warfare unbearable, the cold was inclined to drive men to suicide. Thick, glutinous, fishy-smelling whale oil was used to combat trench foot.

In early December the 16th Division was transferred to Gough's 5th Army. The 49th Brigade headquarters oscillated between various châteaux around Amiens and further to the rear while ordinary billets in this sector were in an ugly industrial siding called Sainte Émilie—less than two miles behind the front at Ronssoy.

As a day of peace and goodwill to all men, Christmas seemed a farce. There was no fighting but the enemy sent over some of his usual greetings. New Year was also unremarkable apart from the usual horseplay from fresh-faced subalterns just out of school. The New Year did not look promising at its birth and there was still the rest of the winter in the front line to be endured. As far as anyone knew, the war might continue for eternity and, provided they were fit for service, everyone was in it for the duration. 'Roll on duration' was the universal cry.

Better known for being the creator of *Christopher Robin* and *Winnie-the-Pooh*, which he wrote in later life, A. A. Milne had already begun to reveal his talent for rhyming. In 'Gold Braid' he tells the familiar story of journeying back to the front after a spell in Blighty. He finds new faces in his platoon, but not much else changed:

> *Same old trenches, same old view,*
> *Same old rats as blooming tame,*
> *Same old dugouts, nothing new,*
> *Same old smell, the very same,*
> *Same old bodies out in front,*
> *Same old strafe from two to four,*

Same old scratching, same old hunt,
Same old bloody war.

The 16th Division was totally reorganized at the beginning of 1918. General Hickie had fallen ill and was replaced by General Sir Amyatt Hull. Its Irish identity disappeared since later conscripts were not Irish. The raw material to be trained was becoming steadily worse. Most of those who joined now came unwillingly although conscription was never introduced in Ireland. What in earlier days had been drafts of volunteers, were now droves of victims. The depleted battalion was strengthened by an intake of mostly undersized 'bantams' barely capable of carrying their own packs.

After the fierce winter, the weather in early March was comparatively mild, bright sun all day and a sharp frost at night. All was quiet but rumours were rife of an impending attack by the Germans. Having grown complacent in their defensive role, the men looked forward to giving the enemy a warm reception. Their confidence stemmed from the belief that it was better to defend than to attack, but the suspense was palpable.

Four months had passed since Harry first applied for compassionate leave, and in mid March he was informed that the brigade HQ had received the permit. Without delay, he rode to their office and saw the brigadier. His advice was 'get away—and tonight'. Disinclined to question such an order, Harry returned to his quarters, handed over his heavy kit to the QM to be dispatched at a later date, and with the yellow warrant in hand, rode off to the rail head with the few things he required for his journey across the channel. He did not see his heavy kit again. Within a few days of his departure, the divisional sector was overrun. News of the massive German onslaught greeted him on his arrival in London.

At once, he reported to the War Office expecting that all officers would be recalled to France but was informed that all leave already granted was to be completed. On the other side of the channel, however, men were turned away from the leave boats. Newly arrived conscripts and men who had never wielded a weapon were drawn into the battle known as *Kaiserschlacht* which began on 21 March 1918. Providence had seen to it that Harry was safe on English soil at this critical point in time.

There had been rumours of a coming offensive and this one was preceded by the customary barrage, greater in intensity and accuracy than anything previously experienced. The barrage cut communications and caused many casualties. Gas was also used. Then at 4.40 a.m. on a misty Thursday morning, along a 54 mile stretch, the Germans attacked.

The village of Ronssoy which was held by the 7/8th Inniskillings was attacked from behind. While some units managed to hold on until late in the afternoon, the position was overrun by noon. The German tide rolled down the hill into the rear areas of the 16th Division. Almost all the officers were killed or wounded. By evening, the 49th Brigade existed only on paper.

Visibility was forty yards. The mist caused a feeling of blind helplessness. Being shelled by one's own artillery added to the confusion. It can be said that the men were dazed but there was not total panic. Countless heroic deeds went unrecorded as individuals and groups attempted to fight their way out of the clutches of the enemy. When capture seemed inevitable, Lewis gunners tore their badges off their jackets for fear of reprisal.

Even though the 16th (Irish) Division fought rear-guard actions and counter-attacked, it was criticized for poor performance—it was alleged that the Irish units did very badly and gave up the village of Ronssoy without a fight. But it must be pointed out that they were defending a salient and the enemy got behind them before they knew it. The 6th Connaught Rangers in particular went above and beyond the call of duty. They were ordered to counter attack but when the order was cancelled, the message did not get through to them. Having had the comfort of absolution, given them by their priest, Father McShane, they moved forward to occupy a trench already filled with the dead and their useless belongings. Every attempt to move was met with a withering fire and within the course of a few minutes, there was nothing left of the battalion.

For the next week, the British army was in full retreat. Units were intermingled and mixed up with crowds of civilian refugees. Planes wheeled overhead machine-gunning concentrations of troops. Guns raked the main arteries and the roads were a mess of craters, destroyed vehicles, broken guns, wrecked gun pits and dead gunners. The Hindenburg Tunnel was ablaze, lighting up the sky since it was heavily timbered.

In eight days, a total of fourteen divisions had been reduced to a rabble of dead-beat troops holding a front of only six miles. But in the end, the enemy was a victim of his own success. He had outrun his artillery and on finding stores of food, and more particularly alcohol, he eventually lost the will to fight, even the officers found it impossible to drive their troops out of the wine cellars.

The retreat along the 5th Army front necessitated a general withdrawal. It was more a case of elasticity than a rout—the line did not break. Fresh troops high in morale marched eastwards with a spring in their step. At times like this, the stubborn valour of the British came to the fore. Amiens was saved.

More than 600 artillery pieces were lost, but guns of the 16th Division played a role in stemming the flow, firing over open sights at targets that could hardly be missed. The Germans too, were exterminated in their thousands. The 16th Division was completely destroyed —7,149 were killed, wounded or missing.

In the aftermath, the 16th Division was disbanded, broken up apparently as punishment for 'disloyalty'. On 16 April, a large number of men in the 49th Brigade mutinied in protest. The punishment for mutiny was usually severe but in this case all sentences were suspended. The 7/8th Royal Inniskillings served in the 30th Division until the end of the war, but it was not the same battalion of old. All the officers (except perhaps Quartermaster William Reid) were gone. One of the old originals killed on 27 March 1918, and never found, was Regimental Sergeant Major Robert Dolan who started off as Alex's Company Sergeant Major in 'C' Company, and the two had been hit by the same shell at Guillemont. Aged 36, Dolan was a professional soldier to the core and had served throughout the Anglo-Boer War.

While this was all unfolding, Harry booked his berth on a Canadian Pacific steamer sailing from Liverpool to Port St John on 26 March. The ship was held up in Liverpool docks for several days waiting for the convoy to be completed. Passengers consisted mainly of officers, fresh from the battlefields of Ypres, going on leave to Canada. Everything was run on the lines of peacetime comfort. Harry had a cabin to himself and he recalled: 'At length, we were given permission to sail and we left Liverpool at dawn in company with eleven freight steamers and an escort of destroyers and one cruiser. When we were out of the Irish Channel, our ship which was considerably faster than the freighters was given instructions to go ahead independently of the convoy.'

The Atlantic was moderately calm and beyond a few depth charges being dropped in the sea for practice purposes, the submarine threat was forgotten. Nevertheless the ship maintained a blackout at night. Perhaps their greatest fear was of hitting an iceberg as the RMS *Titanic* had done six years previously at the same time of year.

Memory of the *Titanic* was still fresh in 1918, the legends and indeed some of the passengers from that ship would have been well known to Harry. One of the Reid's extended clan survived the sinking under a cloud of controversy. Sir Cosmo Edmund Duff-Gordon and Lady Lucy Duff-Gordon were prominent members of the landed gentry from Aberdeenshire. Sir Cosmo was known as 'the finest dueller in England' and was the most celebrated member of the 1906 Olympic fencing team. The man's fine reputation was destroyed by the press simply for being aristocratic and alive. He was vilified as a blackguard who bought his way into a lifeboat and then prevented the crew from rowing back to help those in the water. The court of enquiry exonerated him but he became a sad, lonely figure and remained reclusive for the rest of his life whereas he had once been a gregarious person.

As a former member of the South African forces, Harry paid particular attention to the maritime disasters which befell his adoptive nation.

Unsurprisingly, he was unaware at the time of the greatest maritime tragedy in South African military history. More than 600 South Africans, almost all black troops, drowned when the SS *Mendi* was cut in half in a collision with the SS *Darro* on 21 February 1917. The Captain of the *Darro* declined to come to their rescue and the whole incident was hushed up.

By contrast, there was universal shock and outrage at the news that the *Galway Castle* had been torpedoed on 12 September 1918, two days out of Plymouth and two months before the armistice. She took three days to sink and 143 lives were lost. Altogether, eight ships of the Union-Castle Line were lost during the Great War. The illustrious *Kenilworth Castle* was involved in a collision in the English Channel, thirty-five miles out of Plymouth on the morning of 4 June 1918. She collided with one of her escorts, the destroyer *Rival*, cutting off her stern. Everyone assumed that the ship had been torpedoed and life boats were lowered. Since the ship was still moving at speed, two lifeboats came to grief and fifteen people were drowned, some of whom were nurses.

Crossing the Atlantic in 1918 was not as relaxing as it might otherwise have been, but passengers passed the time in the playing of card games—sometimes for high stakes. Harry would never forget the welcome which nature laid on for his arrival in Port St John in the late afternoon: 'The ship anchored in the Bay of Fundy until next morning and during the night, we saw a fine display of the Aurora Borealis or Northern Lights. A curtain of streams of light seemed to be hanging from the sky which constantly and instantaneously changed their position—accompanied by a mysterious rustling noise.' How peaceful it was compared to the man-made displays to which one had become accustomed in France and Flanders.

At Port St John, which was the northern-most port of any decent size, there was a Canadian Pacific Railway terminus. Not many people travelled from here and Harry took the next train to Montreal where he made an onward connection. Although the train was as comfortable as any in England, he could not help noticing a stark difference on the station platforms which were devoid of the bustling crowds of family friends, porters and railway officials. Luggage was forwarded on to one's destination from the dispatch office so that porters were not required.

Travelling across the continent, one heard talk of ranching opportunities for ex-soldiers in the Cariboo district of British Colombia. The Pacific Great Eastern Railway had been partially completed in 1917 and opened up this remote inland area. It had given a boost to cattle ranchers who would no longer have to undertake long cattle drives but it meant the end of the roadhouses which catered for the travellers on the old wagon road. During the gold rush of the late 1850s, mining people had begun to notice the natural meadows on either side of the Fraser River, which made superb grazing. Although Harry did visit this area and played at being a cowboy for a time, he found the beef industry to be the preserve of the mega-ranches—the Empire Valley Ranch and the Gang Ranch for example. The latter controlled almost a million acres and is said to be the largest ranch in the British Commonwealth. It is rugged country, only marginal land was left and few soldier-settlers managed to carve out a place for themselves.

Arriving on the west coast, one could almost believe oneself to be back in rural England. When the mists lifted off the harbour, where the steamers tied up, the lasting impressions were of cunningly constructed waterfronts, large gardens and winding lanes. It was worth the very long journey, but even in this remote corner of the Empire, the European war cast a dark shadow, and in a way the distance made it harder to bear. The Reid family, like so many others, was in mourning. Harry's living presence made for some awkwardness but there was ample opportunity to escape into the mountains and wilderness.

Since many of the residents were ex-army, it followed that their sons volunteered with alacrity at the outbreak of war. Hardly a single family went unscathed. One grieving father was Colonel H. H. Dobbie who resided in the peaceful enclave of Maple Bay. His son, John, was born in India, and like Alex, he had come to Canada to farm. In 1914 he took a commission in the Gordon Highlanders and was wounded during the capture of Ginchy on 6 September 1916. Left on the battlefield for dead, he made his way back to his lines after dark. He recovered from his wounds but thirteen months later, at Broodseinde, a direct hit on his dugout made sure that his line was at an end.

Having had a glimpse of what life might be like in peacetime, Harry resolved to be extra cautious on his return to the front and abandoned his intentions of joining his old commanding officer, Acting Brigadier H. N. Young, who was now with the Sherwood Foresters. As it happened, Young was killed during the last spasm of the war on 25 October 1918 near Le Cateau. Meanwhile, Harry resumed his usual duties and during the advances of late 1918 his task of keeping the troops supplied and finding water for the animals was exceptionally difficult. The Germans destroyed most of the wells—much the same as they had done in German South West Africa.

As the war drew to a close, life seemed more valuable somehow. The days had an ever-intensifying significance. Life was now infinitely preferable to having a place on the Roll of Honour. Soldiers were constantly calculating the risks involved in a particular action. For example, to save the life of a friend, any risk was acceptable, but to take a life, perhaps a one-in-five risk was acceptable. To pay a social visit to HQ was not worth any risk at all, but while out on a leisurely stroll, Harry came close to being exterminated for no strategic or altruistic purpose:

We were advancing through Belgium over flat country, the Germans had reached a slight eminence from which they overlooked our movements. As their flanks would soon be exposed by the general retreat of their armies, it was only a matter of two to three days before they would be compelled to evacuate their position. In the meantime we were billeted in scattered hamlets. To pass the time, I decided one morning to visit the billets of battalion HQ which was about three quarters of a mile from my own. I came through the trees to a long straight road running across flat country. Beyond, in front of me, was a hill on which the enemy was entrenched. It was a warm summer day. Like a Sunday in the country in peacetime, not a sound could be heard. At any moment, one expected to hear the chime of church bells.

Suddenly, a shrapnel shell exploded about 100 yards in front of me, exactly over the centre of the road. The smoke from the explosion hung for a few moments in the still air and then drifted away. Peace and quiet returned. I stopped. It did not seem possible that a solitary officer was being paid the compliment of a shell all to himself. On the right hand side of the road beside me, was a cottage which had previously been shattered by shellfire, behind which I screened myself from enemy observation. Wanting to continue, I pondered the question of continuing my journey, not sure if I was the object of attack. Foolishly, I decided to stand in the middle of the road and test the question. I had not long to wait.

It is said that the approach of the shell that kills a man is not heard by him—and this one I did not hear, it must have exploded above my head. I saw sparks at my feet, flying off the pavé as shrapnel bullets struck the road. Promptly, I regained the shelter of the ruined cottage and waited there with some anxiety. I now realized that I was the object of attack and expected a salvo into my precarious sanctuary. However, there was no more fire. Again, silence reigned. After the lapse of some minutes, keeping the cottage as long as possible between myself and enemy observation, I retraced my steps across country through fields and ditches leaving the road as far on my right as possible.

I mention this incident to show how much depends on fate. This was an occasion when no attack was in progress or any preoccupation to prevent the German battery from taking careful aim at a solitary person entirely for their own amusement. To be killed in a *bona fide* manner was almost acceptable compared to being shot down like a partridge for mere sport. My own part in the proceeding was foolish, quite unnecessary and deserved nothing but adverse comment.

After the armistice, while awaiting demobilization at Boulogne, Harry motored with two friends, in a sturdy Crossley staff car, to the same area where he had previously searched for Alex's body. They took with them a large wooden cross, suitably inscribed, made by the camp pioneers:

> We reached the place, as near as we could determine from the map, where Alex had been killed (J. 7. B. 70. 05), and erected the cross as a memorial. At a later date before leaving France, I visited the British cemetery at Ypres. The cross had been found by the reclamation corps and erected in the cemetery. Although the body had not been found, I was glad to know that the cross had been moved to this official burial ground and Alex's name, rank and sacrifice on the battlefield was not unrecorded.

At this time it could not have been known that the wooden crosses would later be replaced with headstones and that there would be many different cemeteries around Ypres—meticulously kept by the Commonwealth War Graves Commission. One of the objectives of the regimental memorial fund, of which A. D. Reid was the treasurer and secretary, was to erect a memorial stone in the Philosophe cemetery on which all the names of the fallen from the 7th Battalion would be engraved. It appears that the officers were under the false impression that the Philosophe cemetery was the sole preserve of the 7th Royal Inniskilling Fusiliers

London was having its first season in five years and life was festive. It was not unusual to be asked to three or four parties on the same night. Girls and even older matrons had become emancipated but there remained sufficient of the moral restraint of what was considered correct behaviour to make some breeches of it, very romantic and exciting. In both dress and conduct, something was left to the imagination. Generally, a happy time could be spent in post war Britain, but the men from the colonies were keen to get home with minimum delay.

Since Harry was demobilized in Britain, he was technically a civilian when he boarded a Union Castle ship for home. It was overcrowded and unpleasant with four officers in every two-berth cabin. Already, it seemed that there was no appreciation for one's war service. Even the wounded were expected to do fatigues and ship's officers were inclined to order people around. Bugles were blown to summons passengers to dinner and at 10.30 p.m. lights were put out. Numerous complaints were made to the authorities in Cape Town regarding this rude imposition of authority as well as the quality of the food and being crammed below decks in the tropical heat of West Africa. Once in Cape Town, those who had been demobilized overseas found that they were at a disadvantage because they were excluded from the free facilities offered to men in uniform.

CHAPTER 12

'Peace' and the Rand Revolt

Hardship and violence did not end on Armistice Day. The aftermath of the Great War reached far and wide into the future. Irishmen came home to the realization that their sacrifices went unappreciated. Those who had hoped they would be rewarded for helping the crown felt forgotten and betrayed. Even the general public disowned their brave soldiers, while honouring those nationalists who fought for a free and independent Ireland. Unemployment was rife in Great Britain because of the closing of munitions factories and the appointment of women and temporary workers into jobs which the men had left.

Johannesburg too, was full of unemployed men who had thought that the sole qualification for peacetime employment would be a good record of service in the field and a letter of recommendation from one's commanding officer. Harry's personal narrative is, to begin with, as commonplace as it is full of bile:

> It was not unusual for ex-servicemen to be refused reinstatement in the jobs which they left when the war broke out. In South Africa, as in Britain, massive fortunes were accumulated without effort by the most contemptible and repulsive exponents of unscrupulous greed with the assistance of their shirking accomplices of military age. Through exploitation of the war effort, the company which I had worked for before the war had made a colossal fortune for the benefit of three partners—one senior partner and his two nephews.
>
> What retrenchments were carried out by the head office in Port Elizabeth and other branches and subsidiaries of the organization I have no idea, but the Johannesburg branch without a day's notice, sacked eighteen of their personnel all of whom were demobilized soldiers and of whom I was one. We were just a small fraction of the temporary

soldiers returned with the vain and foolish expectation that the promises made to them by their employers at the time of their enlistment would be honoured.

I had come out to South Africa in 1907 as a private secretary to the senior partner and when he returned to London, I elected to stay on at the Johannesburg branch. Unfortunately he departed this life at the beginning of the war [in January 1915] and control fell into the hands of the remaining partners. By all accounts he left generous bequests to some members of his staff. His Godson, Harry Oppenheimer, was left an amount of £500.

Inflation made an appearance and in view of all the adverse circumstances which those of us who had returned to civilian life had to endure, one would have thought that at least three months' notice of the intention to retrench would have been given—especially considering the fact that the firm had acquired huge reserves during the war years.

The chief hatchet-men were two senior managers—one, a coarse-featured man with a heavy jowl and receding forehead, the other a tall thin man with a sneaking manner. At the outbreak of the war, these two men had been in their early thirties, but rather than risk their necks, they transferred to better positions in civil life thereby obtaining increased pay and other emoluments such as the manager's commission on profits. No small item under existing conditions.

Agreement to the action taken by the two managers was no doubt confirmed by the partner of the firm who was at that time in Johannesburg, but it was too much to expect from such types of men that they would guide the partner's judgment and, if necessary, refuse to execute such a contemptible decision.

For some months, I lived in a room about 10' by 9' in a large building of several floors. The ceiling of my room was a wooden one and each morning when dawn penetrated the dingy curtain, I saw an army of bugs swollen with my blood moving up the wall adjacent to my bed towards the ceiling. They remained there during the day to return at night to feast again and add further blood stains to my sheets. Even the insectivorous parasites which I hosted while in the trenches could not compete with these beasties. One bathroom on each floor served all the bedrooms on that floor. All bedrooms were similar to mine, and there were quite a number. Each morning, I spent some time cleaning the bath which had been freely used as a spittoon by the other lodgers.

Poverty is not a pleasant prospect. I was reaching the end of my financial resources and had to steer clear of the social gatherings at the tea rooms in Eloff Street. A friend lent me ten pounds which I stretched to the very limit. As so often happens, when I was at the end of my tether my luck changed, and a man whom I had known casually before the war offered me a temporary job. He had recently opened the local branch of an American organization, said to be the largest producers, manufacturers and distributors of rubber and rubber products in the world. Within a month, my temporary job became a permanent one. In under a year, I was appointed secretary of the South African company and some years later, a director.

There had been a number of attempts by the unions to foment violent insurrection—even prior to the Great War. Now, towards the beginning of 1922, the class war erupted again and the miners of the Witwatersrand embarked on a terrible strike. Owing to the rising mining costs combined with a decrease in the price of gold, the mine moguls pleaded poverty and refused to pay a higher wage for unskilled work which could be done by the natives. The white miners objected to this assault on their privileges and 22,000 miners went on strike. Their ranks were joined by communists, the unemployed and some criminal elements. It soon became a civil war of striking miners, communists and criminals against the government and law abiding citizens.

Mine management and so-called 'scabs' were liable to be attacked on their way to work. Even the wives of strike-breakers were not safe in their homes. This culture of violence could only have come from the cauldron of war. Militia units, referred to as commandos, were formed along military lines. Afrikaners, who made up the great preponderance of the working class, have an inherent dislike of marching and drilling, but the military culture was strong among returned soldiers. Squads of workers could be seen drilling and parading on waste ground in various parts of the city. There was a Sinn Fein Commando, otherwise known as the Irish Brigade and the Irish Regiment. Typically, these were the shock troops of the strikers—but not all were Irish.

Many of the strikers were veterans of the Great War and their military leaders were likely to be experienced officers. They wore badges of rank, and training exercises involved learning how to make bombs and to unhorse mounted troops. Sandbags and trenches appeared in the streets. Rifles and miscellaneous weapons (including at least three machine guns) were distributed. No attempt was made to hide this militancy.

Things turned violent when gatherings were broken up and arrests effected. Martyrs were made of the first three strikers to be killed. In Johannesburg, shops were forcibly closed, cars overturned and the water supply to Krugersdorp cut off. A mine headgear was blown up and a train derailed. It was clear that this was not just labour unrest, it was more like a revolution of communistic ideals. Two communists played a leading role, Percy Fisher, a hot-headed Englishman, was the key man and Harry Spendiff, a veteran of France and Flanders, was his associate. It was whispered that they were in communication with Moscow.

Government was seen to be backing the capitalists in what was effectively a class war. Race was not the divisive factor although there was talk of a 'black rising' causing a number of innocent black people to be killed when they found themselves in the wrong place at the wrong time. The residents of the affluent green suburbs of Parktown and Houghton where insulated from these incidents which took place on the reef.

After a night of manoeuvring into position, the point of no return was reached on the morning of 10 March 1922 when widespread and largely successful attacks were carried out upon police across the Witwatersrand. At the Newlands Police Station, the police were overwhelmed and relieved of their weapons. At Brakpan, about 1,000 strikers attacked the mine. Eight of the defenders were killed. Two officials were reportedly taken into the *veld* and shot. The situation at Benoni was serious, and 200 members of the Transvaal Scottish were sent to the relief of the town. En route, at Dunswart, the train was forced to a halt and in the ensuing action, which lasted a number of hours, the 'Jocks' lost 12 killed and 30 wounded.

As it had been in 1913, the Rand Club became a symbolic target of the strikers. Mine moguls, leading businessmen and war profiteers gathered at the club to await news. It was said that the leaders of the revolt had a list of names identifying a number of the wealthiest citizens. The situation had assumed the form of a mini French Revolution. For a short time, the control of Johannesburg hung in the balance and the inmates at the club were subjected to a morning of apprehension.

All reservists and available troops were called up, and commandos summonsed from country districts. Johannesburg citizens were urged to join defence force units as temporary volunteers. Ex-soldiers, of the type who identified with management, responded promptly to the call. Also, a number of young men of no military experience or training, who had not previously handled a rifle, were bundled into khaki. School cadets were armed and patrolled their school grounds. Although Harry had good reason to be disaffected by the system, he had no hesitation in rejoining his old regiment, the Imperial Light Horse.

All Imperial Light Horse volunteers were sent to the football stadium at Ellis Park which became their headquarters and it was here that one of the worst clashes with the strikers took place on Saturday 11 March 1922. The surprise attack came just as equipment was being issued. The strikers and communists advanced in three separate groups, from the south and east through a slum area of narrow streets. Fences and trees concealed their approach. Ellis Park at that time was a gravelled space of ground, almost circular in shape, surrounded by a bank of rocks and plants, all enclosed by an iron railing. A veritable death trap for a body of men caught between two fires.

The attackers were a mixed force drawn from the Denver and Jeppe commandos. Fortunately the attackers on the east side commenced firing before those on the south side were in position. The ILH numbered only 150 men—half of whom had been issued rifles and ammunition and were ready to beat off the attack. After the initial shock, the men responded. Lying in extended order across the gravelled space of the park, they repelled the first attack before those on the south side were able to add their firepower. Sniping and gunfire continued for about an hour.

A limited counter-attack was led by Major Rennie and the rabble then dispersed into the network of streets behind the park. Two strong parties of strikers were encountered and driven off. According to ILH regimental folklore, the leader of the attackers, Captain Hall MC, was captured by the regimental trumpeter armed only with a pistol. The action lasted only a few minutes. The ILH losses were eight dead and fifteen injured. Most were shot in the first minute—within half an hour of joining up.

Many of the strikers were armed with only hand guns, but had they been properly armed and had the three groups made their attack simultaneously on two sides, probably no one would have left Ellis Park alive. The strikers would have advanced into the centre of town, the Drill Hall would have been occupied and large stores of weapons would have fallen into their hands.

Ellis Park being in a basin was ill-chosen as a base and it seems that the ILH was remiss for not deploying outlying pickets, thereby allowing the strikers to advance unnoticed. There were sentries posted, however, and Harry Reid was one of them:

> On the day of the attack, I and two others, were detailed for sentry duty on the west side of Ellis Park—the opposite side to where the attack came from. Standing on high ground, I had a clear view over the open space to the opposite side beyond which, trees shadowed and obscured the narrow lanes where the strikers had infiltrated and assembled. As soon as the attack commenced, I got behind a tree which afforded me a measure of cover and from this vantage point, I was able to fire over the line of men below towards the attackers on the far side.
>
> Movement behind a tree caught my attention and I fired a shot. Immediately, a figure emerged on hands and knees and with backward glances crawled slowly towards the shelter of a fence. To some extent, he was obscured by the shadows in the lane, but even so was an easy target.

It was like shooting a sitting bird and I did not fire. It occurred to me that he could be a returned soldier who had been thrown out of his job by war profiteers.

The Durban Light Infantry arrived at Ellis Park on Saturday afternoon at which time the tide was turned. General Coen Brits, brought in *burgher* (citizen) commandos from the *platteland* (country districts) and placed them at the disposal of the authorities—although the strikers were half expecting the *burghers* to join with them in the uprising. With the help of aircraft and artillery, the strike on the East Rand and West Rand was quelled—although it had hardly got off the ground in the west. The strikers were driven off Brixton Ridge and they retreated to their last stronghold in Fordsburg where they were surrounded. The Transvaal Horse Artillery deployed on Brixton Ridge overlooking the rebel position and a somewhat decrepit tank, the only one in South Africa, threatened action. When the tank reached Fordsburg dip, one caterpillar stopped working and it spun around in circles.

The use of aircraft was considered by those on the receiving end to be excessive force and the planes were fired on with an assortment of small arms. Captain Carey Thomas, an observer in one of the machines was shot through the heart. Another plane flown by Colonel Sir Pierre van Reyneveld had to make a forced landing.

Johannesburg citizens hid under their beds at the sound of explosions although Harry did come to know one war bride who was unperturbed— having experienced bombing in London during the war. This refined daughter of a clergyman, Beatrice Crosby, had been removed from her English country home to the rough and tumble of the East Rand. During the strike she was legitimately concerned about her ex-RAF husband whose job it was to go underground every day to feed the rats to prevent them from gnawing on the cables.

The Rand Revolt played out in full view of the public. Crowds from Parktown gathered on the ridge to watch the action. On Sunday 12 March, Johannesburg residents woke to the 'dull boom of bombs'—so said the *Rand Daily Mail*. The Brixton kopjes were being bombed from the air. Aeroplanes circled the area occupied by the revolutionaries, spotting for the artillery, strafing and bombing targets of opportunity.

The final shootout occurred in Fordsburg on 14 March. Artillery shells dropped onto the building in which Spendiff and Fischer were holed up. A few stray ones hit Sacks' Hotel and some crashed through the roof of Conry's pharmacy, reducing it to splinters. A machine gun sprayed the sandbag ramparts outside the headquarters with lead, providing cover for the advancing government troops.

Any of the attacking troops who became too nonchalant were punished by snipers. Some of the rebels melted away but others refused to retire or surrender and took the only remaining option. Spendiff and Fischer decided not to allow themselves to be captured. In the press the next day, there was much speculation about how they met their end. One story was that they were shot by comrades wishing to surrender. Another was that it was shell fire which killed them. But now it is generally understood that they committed suicide using their revolvers. Apparently Fischer, on the eve of the assault made out his will leaving assets worth £2,000 to his wife, with a special request that she look after Mrs Spendiff should the latter need assistance.

There had been considerable loss of life—more bloody by far than the war in South West Africa. A total of 687 casualties were recorded. The military and police lost 72 killed and 219 wounded. The striker's casualties were never established but were estimated at 157 killed and wounded. Forty two innocent civilians were killed and 197 injured in the street fighting.

The Rand Revolt was at an end and the strikers went back to work having gained nothing. The war profiteers clung to their vast fortunes. Four strikers were hanged—ostensibly for criminal acts. They went bravely to the gallows, singing revolutionary songs. One of the condemned men called out 'Are we downhearted?' and the refrain was 'I think not'—just as it had been in the trenches. Leaders of the strike had talked about a social revolution, the dawn of a new future, and so it happened that the enemies of Jan Smuts had the satisfaction of seeing him defeated in the 1924 election.

In 1929, the year that the stock market crash plunged the world into the Great Depression, when Harry was well into his forties, his bachelorhood came to an abrupt end. He got an elegant young debutant, a full twenty years younger than himself, into trouble—which is a more discreet way of saying that the mademoiselle was in the family way. This earth-shattering accident sent shock waves through polite society. The unlucky lass, Eustasie Baines, was the daughter of the Chief Magistrate of Johannesburg—chairman of the Johannesburg Country Club. A generation down the line, people would still be tittering about Harry and Stacy's mistake. The end result was an only child—naturally named after Alex.

On making a final pilgrimage to Dufftown in the late 1950s, Harry and his young wife stayed in the Fife Arms Hotel in the square next door to the Commercial Bank. On the east side of the square, were the principle shops with the names McGregor, Gordon, McPherson and McKerrow above their doors. The *Dufftown News* was published every Friday. The editor, George Ingram, wrote up every word including the advertisements. He set up the type on a machine left to him by his father. Once it was delivered to the press agents, he would disappear into the Fife Arms to join the whisky drinkers at the bar.

Harry took Stacy to see Hazelwood and Ardmeallie where a memorial stone for Alex was placed in the family burial ground at Old Marnoch. A highlight of their visit was being invited to tea by Miss Procter who had been a teacher at the Dufftown school and lived in a cottage beside the toll bridge over the Fiddich River. A plate of cold chicken, ham and stuffing was placed before each guest and the table was piled with soda cakes, oven cakes, dropped scones, oatcakes, current cakes, gingerbread and a Scotch bun. A giant salad consisted of lettuce, eggs, tomatoes, radishes and strawberries. For Harry, time seemed to have receded a half century to the years of his childhood when they sat down so early in the afternoon to do justice to this feast.

Bowls remained the favourite recreation in Dufftown, but there would be no bowling on Sunday which was set aside for worship and reflection. In the historic Mortlach church, like most other churches throughout the Empire, the names of the fallen are inscribed on the walls for the congregation to reflect upon. As one historian, J. M. Winter, has observed: 'The names of the dead create another still living history of the Empire, and disclose a moment when family history collided with world history, leaving traces, indelible traces, which we can see to this day.'

Today, the forgotten little cemetery at Philosophe in France is surrounded by industrial squalor, far off the pilgrimage trail. It is gratifying therefore, that the name of Lieutenant-Colonel A. D. Reid DSO is immortalized on the Menin Gate at Ypres—together with more than 54,000 others from the British Diaspora who died thereabouts and have no known grave. It can now be said of each one, 'he is not missing; he is here'. Large crowds gather under the enormous arch every evening at eight o'clock for a short ceremony. Buglers play the last post and the name of one of the fallen is read out, followed by a minute's silence.

Alex's name is engraved in stone, gilded on wood and lives on in successive generations of Reids. As one of those left to grow old, Harry became wearied by age and condemned by the years. He is remembered for being a dour disciplinarian and a bit pompous. His grandchildren, who grew up knowing nothing of the horrors he had seen, kept a cautious distance, and he was left alone with his memories and his nightmares. Occasionally, he might see the shape of a mutilated corpse in the blackened stump of a tree, or a hand protruding from under the soil with fingers pointing accusingly at ignorant or indifferent passers-by.

And still they come and go; and this is all I know –
That from the gloom I watch an endless picture show,
Where wild or listless faces flicker on their way,
With glad or grievous hearts I'll never understand
Because time spins so fast, and they've no time to stay
Beyond the moment's gesture of a lifted hand.
From: Picture show by Siegfried Sassoon, 1919.

Endnotes

Introduction

1. Unpublished diary of A. D. Reid, Major A. D. Reid—Major R. Lynche-Blosse, 7 August 1916, James Bourhill Collection.
2. P. Fussell, *The Great War and modern memory*, Oxford University Press, New York, 1989, p. 311.
3. G. L. Mosse, Two World Wars and the Myth of the War Experience. *Journal of Contemporary History*, (21) 4, 1986, p. 497.
4. 'Thoughts that you've gagged all day': Siegfried Sassoon, W. H. R. Rivers and '[The] repression of war experience', pp. 219-229. In P. J. Quinn & S. Trout (Eds.), *The literature of the Great War reconsidered—Beyond modern memory*, Palgrave, Basingstoke, 2001.
5. http://www.firstworldwar.com/features/satirical.htm.
6. E. Blunden, *Undertones of war*, Penguin, London, 1928. Introduction by H. Strachan.
7. S. Sassoon, *Memoirs of an Infantry Officer*, Faber & Faber, London, 1974; E. Blunden, *Undertones of war*, Penguin, London, 1928; R. Graves, *Goodbye to all that*, Penguin, New York, 1960.
8. C. A. Cooper Walker, *The Book of the Seventh Service Battalion, The Royal Inniskilling Fusiliers from Tipperary to Ypres*, Naval and Military Press, Uckfield, East Sussex, (reprint) 2002, (original)1920.
9. A. Boden, *F. W. Harvey, soldier, poet*, Stroud, Gloucestershire, revised edition, 1998.
10. J. M. Winter, *Sites of memory, sites of mourning*, Press Syndicate of the University of Cambridge, Cambridge, 1995.
11. A. Thomson, Memory as a battlefield: Personal and political investments in the national military past. *Oral History Review* (22) 2, 1995, pp. 55-73.

12. G. L. Mosse, Two world wars and the myth of the war experience, *Journal of Contemporary History*, (21) 4, 1986, pp. 491-513; J. M. Winter, *Remembering war: The great war between memory and history in the twentieth century*, p. 6; W. E. Lee, Mind and matter—Cultural analysis in American military history: A look at the state of the field, *The Journal of American History* 93, 2007, pp. 1116-1124.